The Complete
PONY BOOK

The Complete
PONY BOOK

Toni Webber

WARD LOCK

© Toni Webber 1985, 1990

First published in paperback in Great Britain in 1990
by Ward Lock Limited, Artillery House, Artillery Row,
London SW1P 1RT, a Cassell Company.

Line drawings by Kevin Maddison

Photographs by Peter Loughran except for
p. 28, Leslie Lane, and p. 148, John Elliot.
The publishers would like to thank
Radnage House Riding School, Radnage
Bucks for their help with the pictures
on pp. 12, 32, 84, 160-61, 169, 172, 173, 176, 177;
they would also like to thank Gary S. Gray
for his help with the picture on p. 172.

Text set in Palatino
by J & L Composition Ltd, Filey, N. Yorks

Printed and bound in Italy
by Canale

British Library Cataloguing in Publication Data
Webber, Toni
    The complete pony book.
    1. Ponies——Juvenile literature
    I. Title
    636.1'6   SF315

ISBN 0–7063–6865–7

Contents

Introduction 7

Part I **First Pony**

1 Learning to ride 10
2 Choosing the right pony 20
3 Keeping a pony in a field 27
4 Essential equipment 34
5 Feeding and general care 50
6 Clothing for rider and pony 59
7 Shows and gymkhanas 63
8 The pony's health 70

Part II **Competition Pony**

9 Choosing a second pony 78
10 Stabling 82
11 Feeding 87
12 Essential equipment 91
13 Schooling and jumping 115
14 Shows and competitive events 130

Part III **First Horse**

15 Choosing the right horse 146
16 Stabling 151
17 Stable routine 157
18 Feeding the stabled horse 164
19 Careers with horses 169

Appendices

I Mainly for parents 178
II The Pony Club 184
III Standard abbreviations used in advertisements 185
IV Useful addresses 186

Index 188

For Charlotte and *her* succession of ponies – Hannibal, Smokey Joe, Bowsy and Minnie – and for Katie, Penny and Lucy and *theirs* – Dusty, Rocky, Snowy, Tammy, Toby, Bowsy, Dillon, Sandy, Andy Pandy, Brandy, Solly, Andy and, of course, Gumboots.

Introduction

Children grow out of shoes and skirts, jackets and jeans. Unfortunately, they also grow out of ponies, and these are much more expensive and harder to replace.

The relationship between a child and her pony may take several months to develop, and it invariably seems to happen that, just when everything is going swimmingly, the rider grows six inches or jumps herself out of the novice classes. The search for another pony is on, and, once found, the slow build-up of understanding has to begin all over again.

If you and your family are first-time pony owners, this can come as a terrible shock. It is difficult to accept that no two ponies are alike, or that what may be the perfect pony for one child might be all wrong for the next. A young rider's tastes change: gymkhana games may be her sole interest one season but the following year she is keen only on eventing or show-jumping. If she is lucky, her gymkhana pony is versatile enough to cope with all forms of competition. If not, a new pony is the only answer.

When I was a child, the range of riding activities available to the ordinary pony owner was fairly limited. Gymkhanas provided the thrills and some children competed in minor show-jumping classes, but cross-country events and dressage for juniors were unheard of and show classes were for miniature Thoroughbreds (or so it seemed) and not for the rough-coated native ponies most of us owned. Our ambitions, in consequence, were small, and many of us kept our ponies until long after we had grown up. My own pony, for example, lived with us for twenty-four years until he died at the age of thirty-two.

My daughter, in contrast, is now fourteen years old. She has been riding for eleven years and in that time has owned four ponies, all except one of them admirably suited to the stage of riding she had reached. I know from experience what it is like to wonder whether the newest pony was the right choice, to hope, when things were going wrong, that another month or two would make all the difference, to realize sadly that the current pony will be too small by the end of the season or lacks the scope to keep up with the level of competition.

This is why I have written this book. To be forewarned is to be prepared. Owning a pony is fun as well as hard work; it provides moments of great elation and excitement as well as sadness and disappointment, although, fortunately, the good times usually heavily outweigh the bad.

But sooner or later you will be faced with exchanging one pony for another. In this book, I have tried to help you to recognize when this moment comes and to give you some idea of what you are letting yourself in for when you become the owners of not one but a succession of ponies.

Toni Webber

Part I
First Pony

CHAPTER 1
Learning to ride

It is a matter of choice which you do first: learn to ride, or get your own pony. If you are wise, you will learn to ride first. Then you can enjoy your pony to the full once you have acquired him. Some families, however, like the idea of having the pony available for a child to learn on. But this works on the whole only when other members of the family know how to look after a pony, or when you know of someone else – the daughter, say, of a knowledgeable friend – who can help to keep the pony regularly exercised and properly cared for.

Nevertheless, there are situations where it would be madness not to buy the pony first; such as when the perfect schoolmaster becomes available and, unless you jump in quickly, the pony will go to another child. Even then, the parents must be able to keep him, virtually as a pet, during the months, or even a year or two, before his new young owner is ready to cope with him all by herself.

Most of you, no doubt, will learn to ride first. This is best done at a reputable riding school, preferably one which has an indoor school for training sessions but which also takes its pupils hacking from time to time. There is almost certainly one in your area, and if you have a choice ask around before you ring up for an appointment. Word-of-mouth recommendation is important.

Equally important, you and your parents should pay a visit to the school before booking a lesson. Your visit should include a tour of the stables so that you can see the conditions in which the ponies are kept. Loose boxes should be light and airy, with good thick beds of straw or shavings and no sign of stale droppings. The stables need not be sparkling with new paint (better that the school should spend more on good-quality food for the ponies than on window-dressing to impress clients) but they should have an air of cleanliness and caring about them. The tack room should be tidy, with the saddles and bridles clean and well-kept, and the food store should be dry, the floor swept and the feed kept in vermin-proof bins.

Most revealing of all are the ponies themselves. Contented, well-fed ponies take an interest in the things going on around them and your visit (unless, of course, it is at feeding time) should bring heads peering over stable doors, ears pricked and eyes bright and alert.

Before finishing your tour of the stables, you should look at the muck-heap. A conscientious owner of a well-kept stable will also have a well-kept muck-heap. This means one that is properly squared off with a flat top and no soiled straw or old dung scattered in the yard.

Ask if you can sit in on a lesson. If the instructor has a recognized teaching qualification (in the UK this is a British Horse Society Assistant Instructor's (BHSAI) certificate), it does not, of course, mean that she is necessarily a good instructor; but it does ensure that the standards of riding she teaches and the methods she uses are recognized. Only observation will give you a hint as to how skilful she is and how enjoyable she manages to make her lessons. A good instructor should build up an understanding between herself and her pupils, so study the reactions of the children taking part in the lesson you are watching. Do they respond well to her orders, does she joke with them, does she vary the tone of her voice according to which child she has to correct or give orders to? Does she shout too much, or not enough? And if they do something wrong, does she pick it up quickly and make certain that the fault is corrected?

When you are satisfied with all that you have seen, then is the time to book a lesson or, more probably, a series of lessons.

The complete beginner will almost certainly have the first one or two lessons on the lunge. This means that the instructor holds the pony on a long rein, while pony and pupil circle around her. From this distance, she can observe the rider's position in the saddle and the way the reins are being held. She can give instructions and observe how they are carried out. And all the time, the beginner knows that the pony cannot run away, so she can concentrate on riding correctly.

Once the instructor is satisfied with the pupil's progress, the lunge rein will be put away and pupil and pony can join a regular class.

This chapter covers much of what you will be taught by your instructor. It is not a substitute for a good teacher, but it will help you to remember what you have been taught.

THE FIRST LESSONS

Approaching the pony

One of the most important lessons you learn when you first start to ride is how to go up to a pony. A pony's natural instinct, if something frightens him, is to run away. However, they are, or should be, taught to trust human beings, so that they know that when humans are around there is no need to feel afraid. Young ponies may react quite sharply to something new although after a while, especially when they see that the human being is calm and unafraid, they forget their own fear. Wise, experienced ponies take most things in their stride, and these are the sort of ponies that should be ridden by beginners.

Nevertheless, you owe it to the pony, however old and wise, to treat him sensibly. Approach him from the front so that he can see you coming, and let your movements be unhurried. You may be eager to sit on his back for the first time, but spare a moment to stroke his nose or neck and to say 'Hello'. Your voice, in fact, is a very useful aid and it is surprising how often beginners – and

indeed more experienced riders – forget that a conversation helps to build up trust between rider and pony.

Never rush up to the pony, especially from behind. At best, you might make him jump. At worst, he could kick out, and a kick from a pony can be very painful.

Mounting and dismounting

First check that the saddle girth is tight enough to prevent the saddle from slipping round when you put your weight in the stirrup. See that the stirrup-irons are down on both sides. You can adjust the leathers approximately to the correct length before mounting by placing the knuckles of your right hand on the stirrup-bar and altering the leathers until the bottom of the stirrup-iron reaches your armpit.

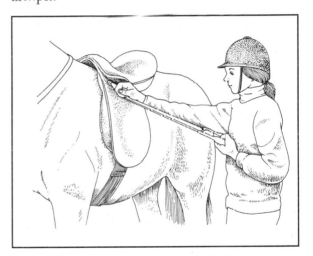

Checking the length of your stirrup-leathers before mounting.

The correct side from which to get on is, by tradition, the pony's left side, known as the *near side*. Stand by the pony's shoulder, take the rein by the buckle in your right hand and draw up the slack. Grasp both sides of the rein in your left hand at a point where the hand can rest lightly on the withers just in front of the saddle, and toss the loop of the rein over to the far side, known as the *off side*. Now, facing the pony's tail, put your left foot in the stirrup-iron and grasp the back of the saddle with the right hand. Spring upwards off your right foot, press the ball of the left foot down into the stirrup-iron, and swivel round as you do so, taking care that your toe does not dig the pony in the ribs. Straighten

Always visit a riding school before you arrange to have lessons there. Here, young riders line up while their instructor checks each pony in turn.

1 Preparing to mount. Stand facing the rear of the horse and gather up the reins in your left hand. **2** Place your left foot in the stirrup-iron and grasp the back of the saddle with your right hand. **3** Press down in the stirrup-iron and swing your free leg over the back of the saddle.

your knees and swing the right leg over the saddle without brushing the pony's loins, then lower yourself gently into the saddle. Place your right foot in the stirrup-iron and take up the reins in both hands.

The process of mounting should be as fluid and easy as possible, aimed at giving the pony the least discomfort. Try not to thump into the saddle, and make the time when all your weight is on one side as short as possible.

Dismounting is easier. Place your reins in your left hand and take both feet out of the stirrup-irons. Hold the pommel of the saddle with your right hand and swing your right leg over the saddle and slide to the ground, landing by the pony's shoulder. You should bend your knees on landing to absorb the jar. Take hold of the reins near the bit and stand by your pony's head.

If you have a whip, this should be held in the left hand, with the reins, for both mounting and dismounting. It is useful to practise these movements on both sides of the pony. In due course, when you start taking part in gymkhanas and other competitions, it saves time if you can mount or dismount with equal fluency from either side.

Your seat
Sit in the centre, or lowest part, of the saddle with your hips square and your back straight. Look towards the front over your pony's ears. Feel that your seat bones are in contact with the saddle.

saddle. Nevertheless, to start with, it is important that you should feel comfortable.

A good position is one in which an imaginary line, at right angles to the ground, passes through your ear, shoulder, hip and the back of your heel.

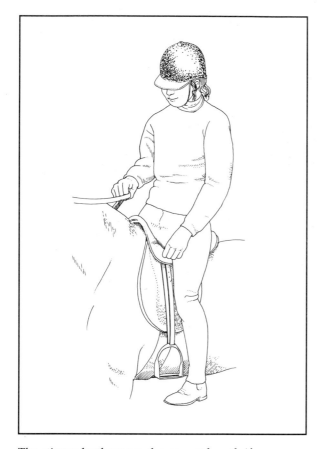

The stirrup-leathers are the correct length if the bottom of the stirrup-iron is level with your ankle bone.

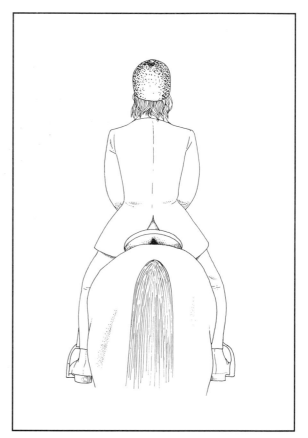

Always sit square in the saddle.

Before moving off, make certain that the stirrup-leathers are adjusted correctly. Take both feet out of the stirrups and let your legs hang down in a relaxed way. Your stirrup-leathers are the correct length if the bars of the irons are level with your ankle bones.

Beginners often complain that their leathers are too long, and shorter stirrups certainly give the illusion of greater security and better balance. As your riding improves, however, you will find that you need longer leathers to make your lower leg more effective. Short leathers tend to push you too far back in the

Holding the reins
Pick up the reins in both hands so that each side passes directly from the bit between the little and third finger, across the palm and out over the index finger, turning your wrists so that the thumbs are on top. Take up enough rein to maintain a light contact with the pony's mouth and allow the loop of spare rein to hang down on the near side. The elbows should be bent sufficiently to form a straight line along the forearm, wrists, hands and rein to the bit, whether it is viewed from above or from the side.

In a good position, an imaginary line, at right-angles to the ground, should pass through your ear, shoulder, hip and the back of your heel.

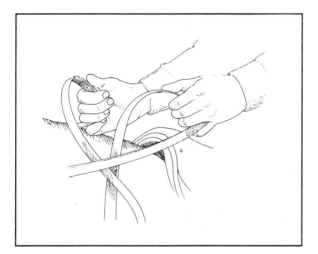

The correct way to hold the reins.

The rein and the fore-arm should form a straight line

The paces

The pony's movements are known as the paces. Each pace has its own sequence of footfalls (see drawing overleaf) and a special term is used to describe it. The **walk** in which the four feet follow one another in turn, is called four-time. The **trot**, in which one diagonal pair of feet hits the ground together, followed by the other pair, is a pace of two-time. The **canter** has three beats, one diagonal pair coming to the ground together, and is known as three-time. In the **gallop**, although it is an extension of the canter, the diagonal pair of legs split slightly into separate footfalls so the gallop is termed a four-time pace.

The paces and your position

The walk Your seat at the walk is the same as when the pony is standing still, except that

Always present a titbit to a pony on the flat of your hand. Even the best of ponies can mistake your finger for something good to eat.

Opposite: A kind pony is essential for a young rider. This rider has complete confidence in her mount, yet her legs barely reach the bottom of the saddle flap.

your body moves slightly at the waist and hips in time with the pony's movement. A pony's head and neck nods rhythmically as he walks and you, in turn, follow the rhythm with your elbows and shoulders. All the time, you should aim at keeping an even, light contact with the pony's mouth. Unless you let your hands give with the movement, you will

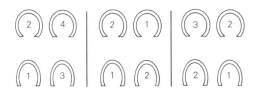

Sequence of footfalls. **Left** The walk (four-time). **Centre** The trot (two-time). **Right** The canter (three-time), shown here for a canter to the left. The diagonals are reversed for a canter to the right.

confuse the pony by pulling him repeatedly in the mouth.

The trot This is the pace that most beginners dread, usually because they have heard how difficult it is from other learners who have already been through the mill. In fact, like so many other aspects of learning to ride, the rising trot is a matter of practice, and it is intended to keep rider and pony balanced and in harmony.

When a horse trots, he moves his two diagonal pairs of legs alternately. The action is bouncy and, at first, you will no doubt feel that you are being joggled right out of the saddle. To compensate for the bounciness and to make the pony feel comfortable at the trot with someone on his back, the rider rises out of the saddle as one pair of legs comes to the ground, and returns to the saddle in time with the other pair.

At first, you will probably find that by keeping one hand on the pommel of the saddle, you can push yourself up in time with

Turning right. Feel the right rein and relax the left sufficiently for the pony to be able to bend his neck as he turns.

Turning left. Use the opposite aids. Always remember that once the pony has obeyed your signal, you should stop applying that particular aid.

The rising trot, right diagonal, rider sitting.

The canter, with the rider sitting deep in the saddle.

the pony's movements. To start with, you will also tend to hollow your back and stick out your tummy. As you grow more proficient, however, you will no longer need the steadying hand and you will be able to keep your back straight. A slight forward movement of the upper body, from the hips, is necessary to keep you balanced, but the weight on your stirrup-irons should remain

the same and your lower legs should stay as still as possible.

Once you have mastered the rising trot, remember to change the diagonal occasionally. This means that you miss a beat: for example, if you are sitting in the saddle when the horse's off-fore (front right) and near-hind (back left) legs come to the ground, you are on the *right diagonal*; if you sit for two beats then rise again, you will return to the saddle when the opposite pair of legs come to the ground, and you are on the *left diagonal*. This variation from time to time is kinder to the pony, especially if you are doing a great deal of trotting.

The canter This is a much easier pace for the rider to cope with than the trot. At a canter, a horse's stride has three beats, and you should stay in the saddle all the time. Try to keep your body supple and your shoulder and elbow joints mobile in order to absorb the beats and the movements of the pony's head and neck. If your back is too stiff, you will bump up and down in the saddle, which is very uncomfortable for both you and your pony.

The gallop This is a faster version of the canter but is ridden in a slightly different manner. The rider needs to get her weight further forward in order not to lose balance or get 'left behind'. This is done by shortening the reins so that the straight line from the elbow through the hand to the horse's mouth can be kept, leaning forward and taking the weight out of the saddle. If you shorten the stirrup-leathers slightly, it will help you to transfer your weight to your knees and stirrups.

The gallop. The rider's weight is now forward on the knees and stirrups.

All these things will be taught to you at a good riding school, and as your competence increases so will your confidence. Soon the time will come when you feel ready to cope with a pony of your own. But even then, it is sensible to continue to have a lesson from time to time. It is much too easy to slip into bad habits unknowingly. A good rider should never stop trying to improve.

CHAPTER 2
Choosing the right pony

You have completed your series of riding lessons. You have acquired the skills necessary to handle a pony both in a school and out on a ride. You have probably learned to remove a saddle and bridle and, if the riding school you went to was a good one, you no doubt know how to put a saddle and bridle *on*. No wonder you have been badgering your parents for the last six months to get you a pony of your own.

At last, the firm 'No' has passed through the 'Maybe' stage and reached a committed 'Yes'. So now you are looking for a pony.

It is important that you realize straightaway that you are still learning. There are many aspects of owning a pony which never arise while you are still at the riding school. The most important of these is responsibility. When an animal is dependent on you for its welfare, you have taken on a duty which can *never* be shirked. However much you might want to join your non-riding friends for an outing to the local swimming-pool or ice-rink, you cannot go until you have completed your duty to your pony.

Fortunately, most pony-owners undertake this responsibility both willingly and eagerly. You will be rewarded a hundred times over by the fun and companionship that a pony brings, but you may have to make some sacrifices. It is best to be aware of this at the outset.

Now for the pony itself. A first pony must be reliable, kind, generous and willing. It must give you confidence because there will be plenty of times when you have to cope with it on your own, with no comforting riding instructor around to help you. If your parents are totally ignorant of horses, you will be the only 'expert' in your household.

The choice of a first pony must therefore be made with extreme care.

FINDING A PONY

Ponies are bought and sold in four different ways: by word of mouth; through advertisements in riding and local papers; through a dealer; and at auction.

Word of mouth

This is clearly an excellent method of finding a suitable pony. Your best plan is to tell your friends that your parents have finally agreed to get you a pony. Ask if they know of anyone who is looking for a likely buyer. If you are lucky, the word will come back that someone is selling their child's first pony because she is now going on to something bigger, and they would be only too pleased to let you try it because it would save them the bother of having to advertise.

Advertisements in papers

This is the most usual market-place for horses and ponies and you only have to look at the small ads section of any of the riding magazines to realize that hundreds of ponies change hands every week. It has its risks though. A pony's good points will be emphasized in the advertisement, but it is up to the prospective buyer to discover its faults. Advertisements also have their own jargon. 'Bombproof' should mean that the pony is generally unflappable, even when it meets a combine harvester or a fleet of motor-cyclists. 'Quiet to catch, shoe, box, clip' means that it is reasonably easy to catch when it is loose in a field, that it is not afraid of the farrier, that it will go in and out of a trailer without fuss and that it doesn't mind having its coat clipped. 'A real confidence-giver' should mean just what it says.

'Not a novice ride' would be an unlikely candidate for a first pony. It could mean that it is a lively pony; on the other hand, it could be a polite way of saying that it 'bombs off' at the slightest provocation.

Through a dealer

This is often a good way of buying a pony, although it won't be the cheapest. The dealer has to earn his living, after all. A good dealer, with a reputation to keep up, will go to endless trouble to find the right pony for you and will often agree to take it back if it proves unsuitable. Sometimes a dealer may be able to offer you the choice of three or four ponies. It is important, however, that you know *exactly* what you want. Do not be tempted to exaggerate either your ability or your experience.

At an auction

This is the place to get a pony fairly cheaply, but it is fraught with hazards. For one thing, you will not get a chance to try out the pony, although you will be allowed to examine it. It may carry a warranty of soundness but the period of the warranty is likely to be short, possibly only twenty-four hours. If you are considering visiting an auction sale in your search for a pony, it is absolutely vital that you go with someone who has had many years' experience with ponies.

WHAT TO LOOK FOR

Temperament, age, size and conformation are the four most important considerations in choosing a pony.

Temperament

This means the way in which the pony behaves, and it can make all the difference between a pony which is absolutely right for you and one which would be better with somebody else. You, too, have a temperament and if yours and the pony's match then you have the perfect combination. So be honest with yourself. If you are nervous, admit it. If you really prefer to go slowly and stay at the back of the ride, look for a pony which shares your attitude. If you are a day-dreamer, look for a sure-footed pony which will carry you safely however much your mind wanders. If, on the other hand, you like to lead the way and are always the first over a jump or into an adventure, you will need a bold, forward-going pony which is happy to take the lead.

The best way to find out if the pony you are trying out is the one for you is to ask. It is very difficult for anyone asked a direct question to answer with a barefaced lie. On the other hand, if you don't ask, the seller may easily forget to give you the information you most need, not necessarily because they want to deceive you but simply because it never occurred to them that you might want to know.

Age

Many people feel that a pony is not worth buying unless it is young, by which they mean five or six years old. Usually, they are thinking of the time when they will have to sell the pony themselves, when it will be two or three years older and perhaps harder to sell. It is a great pity that youth has assumed so much importance. The ideal age for a first pony is about fifteen years old or more. By that age, it has learned wisdom and experience and still has ten to fifteen years of honest service to come. The best first pony this author ever knew was still giving confidence to beginners, guiding them through their first gymkhanas and taking care of them on rides at the age of thirty-five.

Certainly, a first pony should be at least eight years old. No pony should be sold to an inexperienced home under the age of four. Between five and eight it may be suitable for a beginner, but the chances are that it is quiet and docile because it is young. Of course, very old ponies will require more looking after and as they grow even older and you grow more ambitious they will not be able to manage the work you want them to do. But by that time, you will no longer be a beginner and it will be time to let the pony go to another novice to start the confidence-giving process all over again.

Size

It is just as foolish to get a pony that is too big for you as to buy one that is too small. Remember that if you are having to look after the pony all by yourself, you must be able to saddle and bridle it and groom it properly without having to stand on a box. You must also be able to get on the pony without the aid of a mounting-block. And it helps if you can vault on bareback.

Most native ponies may be small, but they are strong and sturdy and perfectly capable of carrying an adult. As a rough guide to matching height of pony and age of child, the following table will help.

Pony's height	Age of child
Under 11 hh	Under 7
11 to 12 hh	7 to 9
12.1 to 13 hh	10 to 13
13.1 to 14.2 hh	12 to 17
14.2 to 15.2 hh	15 to 17

A hand (hh) measures 4 in (approximately 10cm) and the height of a pony is taken from the withers, the highest point of its shoulder, to the ground.

Your own build is also important, of course. If you are small for your age, you can keep a small pony for longer than your gangling friends. Your age becomes vital only when you are entering competitions.

Conformation

Conformation means the pony's build. The way a pony is made affects its movements, and faults in conformation can lead to problems in fitting a saddle. But just as you may feel that your nose is too big or your legs too fat and that you would never win a beauty contest, so a pony can have small faults which make it useless for a showing class but do not affect its performance elsewhere.

However, here are some points to bear in mind:

Round, broad-backed ponies can be uncomfortable to ride, especially if you are not very tall. If your legs are stretched wide, you will not be able to give the leg-aids properly and this will make it difficult for you to improve your riding and your pony's ability. You may also have difficulty finding a saddle which fits properly and does not slip.

Short-withered ponies can have trouble with their saddles. A *low wither* may cause the saddle to slip forward and you will need a crupper to keep it in place. *High-withered ponies* can suffer the opposite problem – the saddle slips back or makes the pony sore.

Narrow-chested, flat-ribbed ponies may lack stamina. If their forelegs are too close together, they may not be very sure-footed and therefore may be likely to stumble or even fall.

Thick-necked ponies can be very strong. They may also lean on the bit, which is uncomfortable and tiring for the rider.

Ponies with a low head carriage are also tiring to ride. However, a low head carriage may be due to lack of schooling rather than poor conformation and careful riding can overcome the problem. But for a beginner, it is best to choose a pony with a good head carriage. *A high head carriage* may make the pony difficult

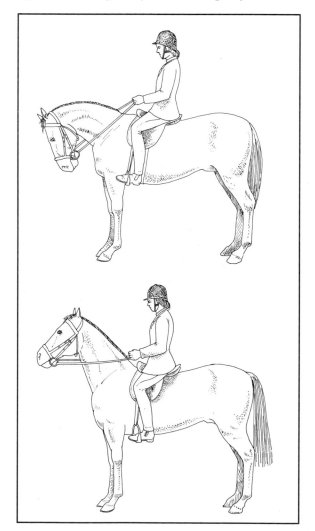

Two ponies to avoid. **Top** The pony is over-bent. By tucking his head in, he is able to evade the bit. Careful schooling, however, could correct this fault. **Bottom** This pony has a heavy head and a short, thick neck. No amount of schooling could correct this fault of conformation.

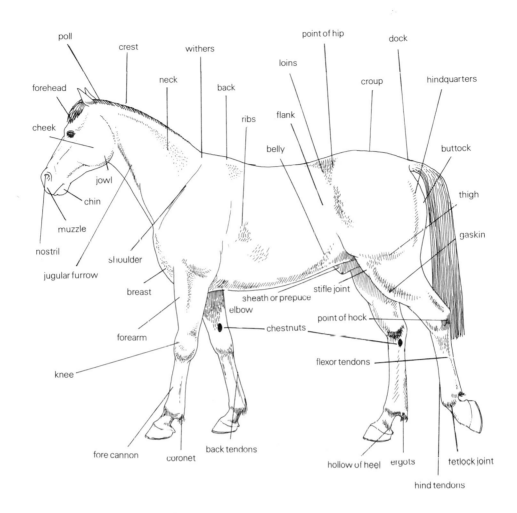

The points of the horse.

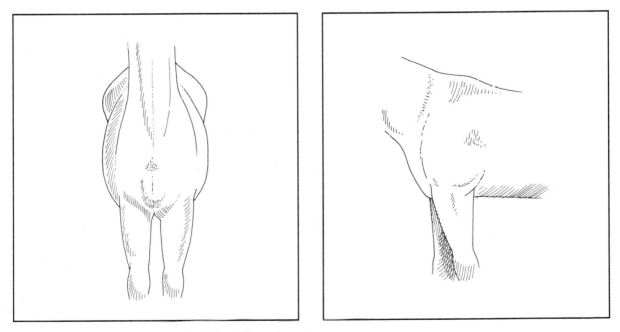

Left A narrow-breasted pony. **Right** A shallow-chested pony.

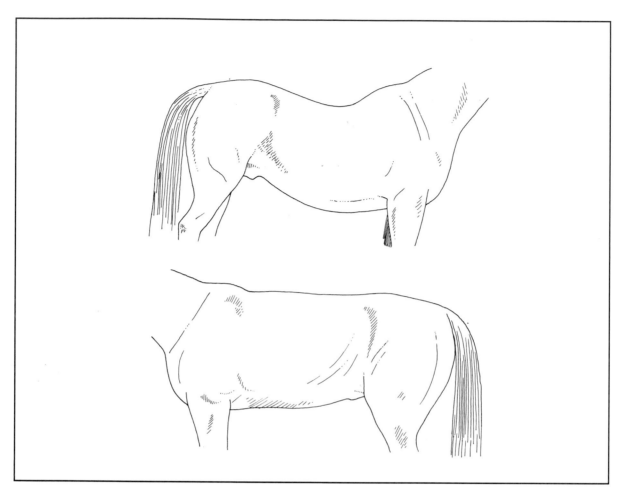

Two more faults to avoid. **Top** A Hollow-back. **Above** A Roach back.

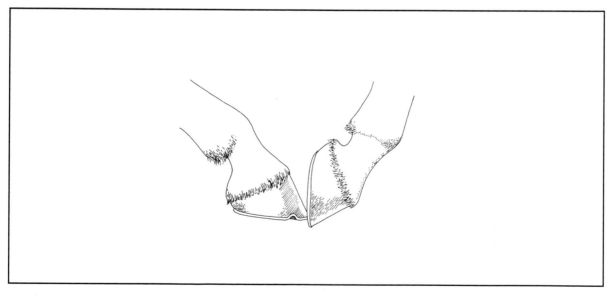

Forging. This happens when the toe of the hind shoe strikes the underneath of the front shoe, making a noticeable clicking noise. It is caused by a weakness in conformation, and the only remedy lies in the shoeing. The blacksmith should be consulted.

to control, particularly if it sticks its nose in the air. Again, it is wise to avoid such a pony if you have very little experience.

Long-backed ponies or those with high-stepping action are uncomfortable riding ponies.

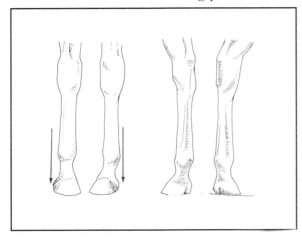

Left Knock-kneed and pigeon-toed. **Right** Cow-hocked.

Cow-hocked or knock-kneed ponies may have an awkward action and there is a danger of the legs interfering with one another. Unless the pony is supremely suitable for you in every other way, you should let your search for the right pony continue.

Of course there is one other factor in all this which will have an effect on the pony you eventually end up with, and that is cost. Study the advertisements to get some idea of the current prices expected for a pony of the type you require. It is only when the pony has had considerable success in competitions that its price is much higher than the average.

GOING TO LOOK AT A PONY

It is probably useless to say to anyone who is going to look at a pony that it is wise not to make up your mind too quickly. Whatever made you decide to go in the first place – the wording of the advertisement, a telephone call from a friend or the horse dealer – you already will have mentally given the pony qualities which have never been claimed by the person who is selling it. You will be 90 per cent certain that this is just the pony for you.

Nothing anyone can say will stop this secret feeling, but do beware of it. It will encourage you to overlook faults and make excuses if the pony does not come up to scratch: 'It doesn't know me. It'll be different when I get it home.' The truth is, of course, that this is unlikely, so be sensible. Take an experienced person with you who can look at the pony with an objective eye.

When you have arranged to visit the pony, try to be there on time; if you cannot make it, telephone the owners to let them know. There is nothing more frustrating for the seller than, after preparing a pony for inspection, she has to hang about for hours waiting for the purchasers to turn up.

It is natural for the seller to want to present the pony in the best possible light, so you will doubtless find it well groomed, with oiled hooves and clean tack. It is rare for the sellers to wait until you arrive before collecting the pony from the field and giving it a quick rub over, before allowing you to try it, although this would give you a very good idea of the pony's virtues. It is helpful, for example, to see how good the pony is about being caught. Otherwise you will just have to ask.

You should take along a list of questions that you have prepared in advance, to put to the sellers when you have tried out the pony. Such a list could include:

Is it easy to catch?

Will it stay in a field by itself?

Is it good-tempered and quiet to handle, especially when eating food?

Is it good-tempered with other ponies?

Will it go well on its own, or does it become nappy when asked to leave a group of ponies? Animals which have been used in riding schools, for example, often become impossibly difficult when they are by themselves.

Will it go into a trailer without fuss?

Is it good in traffic?

Does it behave well with the blacksmith or vet?

Is it head-shy? Some ponies, which have been ill-treated in their youth, object to having their ears touched. This could make things difficult for you when you have to bridle the pony yourself.

You should, if you can, ride the pony before deciding whether to buy him or not. The sellers may suggest that their child or friend puts the pony through its paces first and this will give you a good idea of how the pony goes for someone he knows. But you should also ride him, even though you may make allowances for you and the pony being strangers to each other. You may, for example, find difficulty in getting him to canter, mainly because you are rather inexperienced and the pony knows it. Also try leading him in-hand, and check yourself that the pony doesn't mind having his feet picked up in turn.

On the pony's general suitability and soundness, you should listen to the advice given you by a knowledgeable friend, whose experienced eye may detect faults which are not apparent to you.

While it is a good idea to have the pony checked by a vet before you buy it, it is perfectly possible to spot a healthy pony when you see one.

A healthy pony is alert, bright-eyed and has a shine to its coat. Check that its feet are in good condition. If the hooves are cracked or overlong, it suggests that the present owners have not been taking care of them properly. A heavily ridged hoof is an indication that the pony has at some time in the recent past suffered from *laminitis* (see page 71). An inexperienced owner should avoid a pony which has had laminitis.

Another disease to which some ponies are prone is *sweet itch* (see page 72). This is a skin condition caused by an allergy to biting insects and is apparent only in the summer months. Sweet itch does not occur in the winter months and if you are buying a pony in the early spring there may be no signs of the problem. Always ask about sweet itch. You should not buy a pony which suffers from it unless you have your own stable and field next to your house.

Once you have found the pony which is perfect for you, the time has come to bring it home.

CHAPTER 3
Keeping a pony in a field

A first pony does *not* need a stable. Contrary to what anyone may tell you, a pony's natural habitat is out-of-doors, summer and winter alike. At this stage in your pony-ownership, a stable is an unnecessary luxury.

It does, however, need a secure field with reasonable grazing, a regular supply of fresh water, and some sort of wind-break.

THE RIGHT FIELD

It is not possible to be definite about the amount of grazing a pony requires. Much depends on the size of the pony and the quality and nutritional value of the grass available. As a general rule, however, a single pony needs one to two acres to keep it healthy throughout the year. Supplementary feeding will be necessary in the winter.

Many pony-owners do not have their own field and lucky indeed is the child with access to unlimited grazing. Most children, through their parents, have to rent grazing and this can be an expensive item in the maintenance costs of one pony.

A field next to your house, particularly one which is owned by your family, is the ideal situation. The nearest grazing, available to rent, may be some distance away and this can present problems when feeding in the winter or when you want to ride.

Some farmers are willing to let out a field on a grass-rent basis. This means that you pay rent for the grazing rights, usually on a re-newable lease for a period of one year less one day, with the rent payable quarterly, and no limit to the number of animals you wish to graze on the field at any one time.

Other farmers and land-owners will rent out grazing on the basis of a weekly payment per pony. This is a very common arrange-ment, which can be terminated by an agreed period of notice on either side, normally four weeks or one month. The land-owner is financially responsible for the upkeep of the fencing and the provision of water, but it is your responsibility to see that any repairs are carried out.

The ideal field is about two to three acres in size, with undulating ground, secure post-and-rail fencing, a high hedge to act as a wind-break, and a gravel-bottomed stream, or spring-fed pond, to provide fresh water.

Not many fields reach this ideal, however. Some may be so big that it takes you half an hour to *find* your pony, let alone catch him. Another may be less than an acre in size and must be rested from time to time to help pre-serve the grazing. Water is often mains-supplied, either piped in to an automatic trough or controlled by a tap, from which you will need a hose-pipe to fill a makeshift trough or buckets. If the field lacks any form of wind-break, even a natural hollow in the ground, you will have to supply a field shelter. And the fencing is likely to be barbed wire.

None of this matters too much as long as what you have, you look after properly.

Grazing

Many farmers do not like having horses on their land because of their wasteful grazing habits. Horses look for the tastiest grasses, trampling down other nutritious grasses in the process. Where they have left their droppings, the grass grows coarse and rank, allowing weeds, such as docks, nettles and thistles, to develop. In time, a field which is exclusively and permanently grazed by horses grows patchy in appearance. The ground becomes almost bare in some places and thickly and coarsely grassed in others. If the field is not properly looked after, it will become horse-sick and infested with worm parasites, which in turn infect the ponies grazing on it.

Fortunately, there are various ways in which a small area of grazing can be kept in reasonably good condition. The first is to pick up the droppings regularly and remove them to a muck-heap. This needs to be a daily chore, for even only a couple of ponies can produce a large amount of manure in a very short time.

The second is to rest the field for periods of six weeks to three months. During this time, the field should be topped with a mower, which cuts down the coarse grass and allows the better grasses to grow. Harrowing will also help. It spreads the droppings around (if you haven't had time to pick them up) so that they dry out, and the parasites then die.

Grazing other livestock, such as bullocks or sheep, in the field is extremely beneficial. They eat off the coarse grass and destroy the horse parasites, which cannot harm the sheep or bullocks.

Proper land-care means that you can keep a pony healthy on a smaller area of grazing than would otherwise be the case. Two ponies, for example, can live easily in two one-acre paddocks, as long as each paddock is given time to rest and recover.

Fencing

The most secure form of fencing is post-and-rail, either standing alone or combined with a hedge. It is expensive to buy and erect but it lasts a long time. The cheapest fencing is wire, either plain or barbed. To be secure, at least three strands of plain wire will be needed (four or five are better), properly stretched and fastened to posts set firmly in the ground. The bottom strand should be at least 30cm (12 in) from the ground. Barbed wire is not advisable because it is dangerous if it is not really taut, but for those who have to rent someone else's field there may be no other choice. You must be extra vigilant with

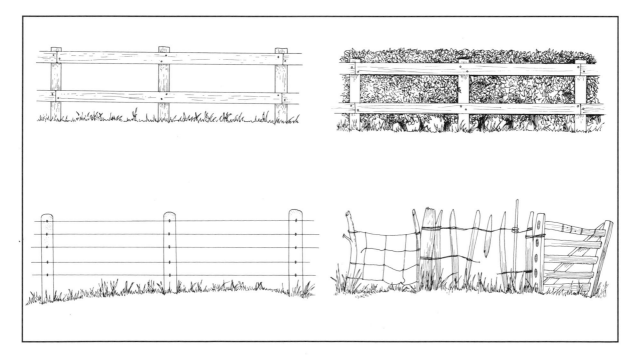

Top left Plain post-and-rail.
Top right Post-and-rail fence, with hedge behind.
Bottom left Plain wire fence, properly erected.

Bottom right Bad fencing. Sheep netting is dangerous as the pony may get his hoof caught in it; chestnut paling may be used if it is protected by a hedge but not alone, as here; the railed gate is too flimsy.

a wire fence of any kind as the wire may become slack and the posts may loosen.

If there is a hedge round the field, it may need strengthening with an inner post-and-rail fence. It is a good idea to allow the hedge to grow high along the side from which the prevailing wind blows as this will provide the necessary wind-break. Always check that there is no yew in the hedge because yew is extremely poisonous.

Gate
A proper field gate is best as long as it swings clear of the ground and the gatepost is firm. The access to the field should be wide enough to allow a tractor through when the field needs cutting, although a narrower gate, such as a hunting gate, would be quite wide enough for ponies. The gate-fastening should be pony-proof, and there are plenty of patent latches and fastenings on the market. Gates, however, do tend to drop in time, making the fastenings difficult to manage. If this happens and the gate cannot be rehung, the safest form of fastening is a chain with a clip or ring through which the other end passes. Baler twine, which goes right round the gatepost and through the gate to be tied in a double bow, is a cheap alternative but not very pretty.

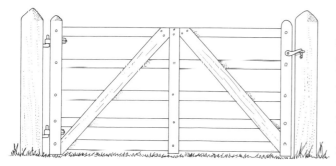

A five-barred gate, well hung.

Water
In the absence of a stream or spring-fed pond, some form of trough must be provided. A stagnant pond, or a stream with high banks or thick mud at the bottom should be fenced off. Automatic troughs are found on most farms that have piped mains water. They are fed by an underground pipe and controlled by a ball-valve which keeps the water at a certain level. Sometimes a tap is used to control the flow of water and, for safety's sake, the pipe leading to the tap should hug the side of the trough. If the nearest water tap is some way away, you will have to buy a hose-pipe to transfer water to the trough.

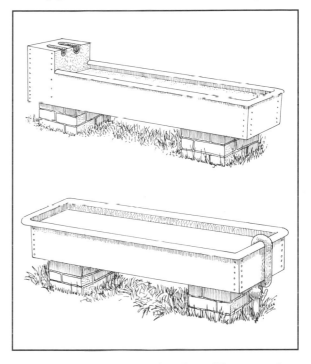

Top Automatic water trough. **Above** Water trough with supply pipe hugging the end of the trough.

From time to time, the trough should be emptied and scrubbed out to remove any algae and scum which has formed. Remember that in winter, the trough may freeze over or the water supply may freeze. In that case, you will have to carry buckets to the field from the nearest house. A rubber ball left floating on the surface of the water helps to keep it free from light ice.

Shelter
Most ponies and horses are unconcerned by rain and snow. They dislike wind, however, and like to stand in the lee of a wall, hedge or building, or even in a hollow in the ground, when a gale is blowing. In summer, they need protection from the hot sun and flies and will chose to stand in the shadow of a tree. If there is no suitable tree available, a field shelter is the answer. This is a three-sided shed positioned so that the opening faces away from the prevailing wind. It

An open-sided field shelter provides protection for both winter and summer.

should be big enough to prevent one pony from being cornered by others in the field. If your field has such a shelter, you will almost certainly find that your pony goes inside it more often in the summer-time.

COMPANIONSHIP

Although many ponies can and will live alone, they are better off in company. They are herd animals by nature and need friends of their own kind. When you get your new pony, you should try to provide him with a companion. Many people share a field with a friend, and this works very well as long as the owner of the other pony is indeed your friend. Your two families can share the responsibilities and costs of feeding, watering and inspecting the ponies, and of maintaining the fencing and the quality of the pasture. There will always be someone nearby who knows your pony and can look after it while you are away on holiday or if you are ill. Best

of all, you have someone with whom to ride and to share the joys of owning a pony.

CHECKING THE FIELD

Before turning a pony out into a field, always make a careful check for safety. Look at the fencing and repair any damage.

See that none of the following poisonous plants are within reach. All parts of the *yew* are dangerous. It is highly poisonous and usually fatal. *Deadly nightshade*, which grows in hedgerows, is also dangerous. *Ragwort*, a tall, yellow-flowered plant, is poisonous when dead. If ragwort is growing in your field, you will spot it during the summer months. Pull it up while it is in full flower and remove it to a bonfire. *Never* leave pulled ragwort lying around on the ground. *Acorns* are harmful if eaten to excess. *Bracken* has long-term ill-effects if it is eaten over lengthy periods of time. Garden shrubs such as *privet* or *laurel* are poisonous, but the dead leaves

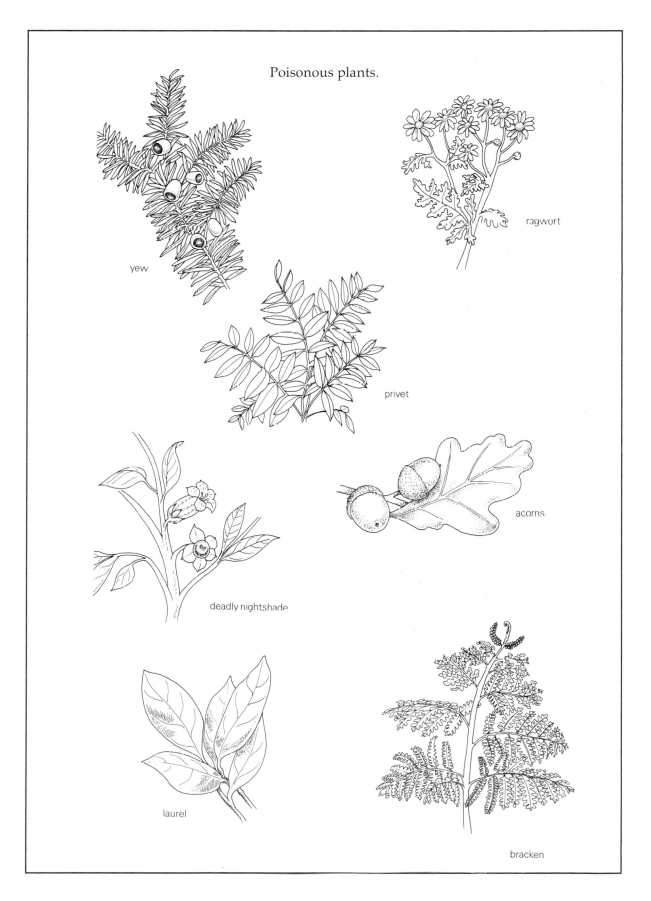

Poisonous plants.

yew

ragwort

privet

deadly nightshade

acorns

laurel

bracken

are more dangerous than the living plants.

If your field is bordered by gardens, do make certain that the householders are not throwing clippings into the field, and warn the neighbours that they should not give lawn mowings to ponies. Their actions, however kindly meant, could make your pony very ill, as lawn mowings ferment quickly.

Finally, especially if a public footpath runs by the field, check that plastic bags, cans and bottles have not found their way over the fence. Cans and broken bottles can cause nasty injuries and a plastic bag is dangerous if the pony eats it by mistake.

TURNING OUT A PONY

The moment when you bring your new pony home for the first time is an exciting one, but do remember that it is bewildering for him. It is rather like starting at a new school, but whereas you have the chance to prepare yourself mentally for the ordeal, the pony has no idea what is happening to him. He started the day in familiar surroundings and now he has been taken to a completely strange place, probably in a trailer or horse-box from which he cannot see out. He may well be used to travelling but, before, he always emerged to the excited sounds of a show or rally.

Give him time to look around and settle down. However much you may be longing to ride him and to show him off to your friends, wait a day or two.

The best time for him to arrive is in the morning, so that he will have many hours of daylight left to explore his new home. This is particularly important if he is to join other ponies in the field. The old hands are sure to crowd round him, anxious to inspect the newcomer, and there will no doubt be some squealing and mild kicking. Normally, the 'getting to know you' routine takes about half an hour. After that, the new pony will begin to graze a little apart from the others. Later on, his place in the pecking order will be established and he will become a recognized member of the herd. He may eventually end up the boss of the field – the smallest ponies are often the bossiest – eating the best hay, having the first drink at the water trough, finishing up the other ponies' food.

It is sensible to leave his headcollar on him while he is turned out in the field, however easy to catch he may be. He has no idea who you are, after all, and may well be reluctant to come to you in the beginning. So be prepared to spend the first few days giving him titbits, catching him, making a fuss of him and letting him go again. You want him to look forward to seeing you. You and your pony are going to be friends and companions, hopefully for a long while, and the relationship should begin on a high note.

Quietly grazing. If a pony is at all difficult to catch, he can always be turned out in a headcollar.

CHAPTER 4
Essential equipment

The longer you have a pony of your own, the more equipment you will acquire. Luckily, a great many items are not necessary immediately, and your family and friends will soon find that choosing birthday and Christmas presents for you will become an easy task.

Some things, of course, are essential from the beginning. The pony – even a first pony – cannot do without: bridle; saddle; headcollar and lead-rope; tack cleaning kit; saddle and bridle racks; grooming kit; buckets.

Let us look at each item in turn.

Plain snaffle bridle, with cavesson noseband.

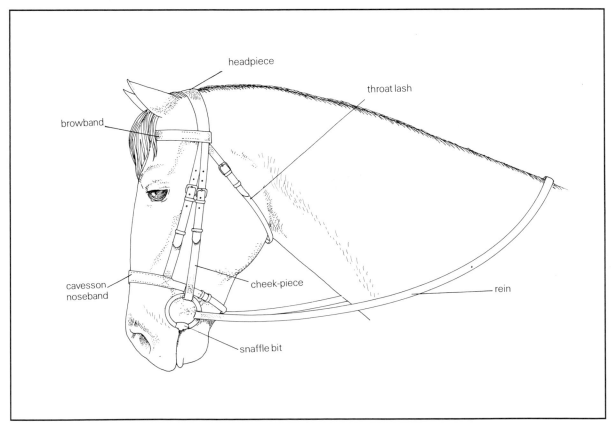

BRIDLE

A simple snaffle bridle should be adequate for your first pony. Bridles are sold in three sizes: pony, cob and full. However, ponies' heads vary in size. If your pony has a large head, and you are buying a new bridle for him, he may need the cob size. If possible, it is best to buy the pony's own bridle when you buy the pony. Even if it is old, it will serve him very well as long as it has been properly looked after.

Most bridles are made of leather. They can be adjusted easily to ensure a good fit, and can be taken apart for cleaning. It is important that you know the different parts of the bridle and how to put it together.

The *headpiece* is a leather strap which passes over the top of the pony's head behind his ears (the poll). It is made in one piece with the throat lash (or latch), which is a longer, thinner strap that comes under the pony's jaw-bone, buckles on the near side and prevents the bridle from coming off.

The *cheekpieces* are buckled to the headpiece and hang down on either side of the pony's face to support the bit. By raising or lowering the cheekpiece, the position of the bit in the mouth may be altered.

The *browband* is a strap with a loop at each end through which the headpiece passes. It runs across the pony's forehead and stops the headpiece from slipping back.

The *rein* is fixed to the bit rings and is usually in two parts, linked by a buckle.

The *bit* on a first pony should be a snaffle, usually jointed in the middle. It should be positioned so that it just wrinkles the corners of the pony's mouth. If it is too low it will

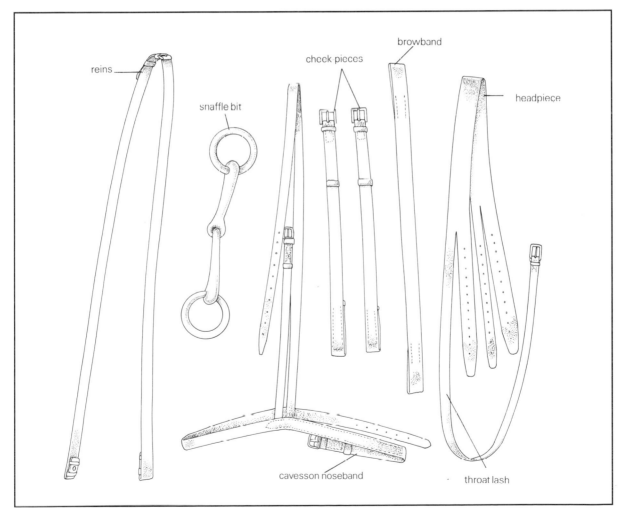

reins

snaffle bit

cheek pieces

browband

headpiece

cavesson noseband

throat lash

The parts of the snaffle bridle.

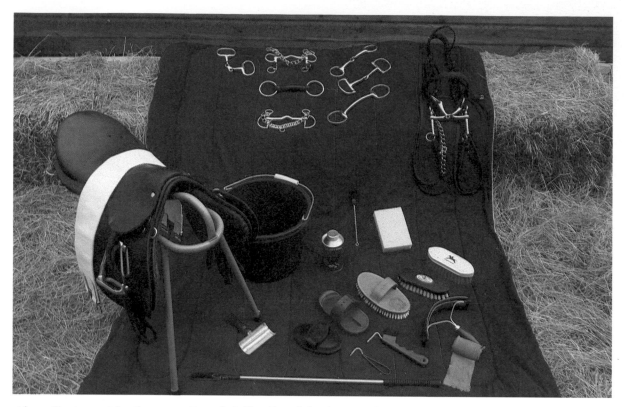

Above Equipment for the pony. **From left** Bits: French bridoon, Pelham, eggbutt snaffle, rubber snaffle, D-cheeked snaffle, Kimblewick, straight-bar snaffle. Double bridle. General-purpose saddle, fitted with safety stirrups. Bucket. Grooming kit: hoof oil, hoof-oil brush, sponge, metal curry-comb, rubber curry-comb, plastic curry-comb, body brush, water brush, dandy brush, two hoof picks, sweat scraper, tail bandage. Whip.

Opposite A first pony should need no more than a plain snaffle bridle, with a cavesson noseband.

bang against the pony's teeth. It controls the pony in two ways. When pressure is put on the reins, it acts on the corner of the mouth and exerts a slight pull on the horse's poll or top of the head. The joint in the middle has a nut cracker action on the tongue. The tongue should lie under the mouthpiece of the bit.

The *noseband*, or *cavesson*, is held in place by a strap which goes over the pony's head, through the loops of the browband, and buckles on the near side. The strap lies under the headpiece. The diameter of the noseband can be adjusted by means of a buckle at the back. A cavesson serves no purpose unless the pony is being ridden in a standing martingale (and no first pony should need such a martingale). In this case the front end of the martingale is looped on to the noseband. The noseband, however, is regarded as important in making the pony look properly dressed.

In Western bridles, nosebands are not used, but then the whole Western style of riding is totally different from the English or Continental style practised in Europe and on the eastern side of America, and so are the saddles and bridles used. It may be tempting to remove your pony's noseband to give him a more real Western look. However, nosebands on their own have a habit of disappearing, and this can lead to disaster at showing time. The easiest way of keeping your bridle intact is never to separate the noseband from the rest of the bridle except when you are cleaning it.

SADDLE

The best saddle for general use is known as a general-purpose saddle. Here again, it is wise to buy the pony's own saddle at the time you buy the pony. However, it is very important for your own comfort and safety that the saddle should fit you as well as the pony. A good saddle carries the rider in the correct riding position without any discomfort to the horse and without forcing the rider's legs forwards or backwards.

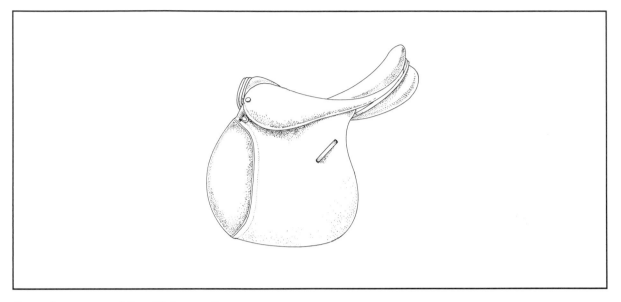

General-purpose saddle with knee roll.

A saddle is made up of several parts.

The *tree*, the skeleton of the saddle, determines the shape of the final product, and is therefore most important. It is traditionally made of laminated beechwood, although modern man-made materials, such as plastic and glass fibre, are used nowadays. A *spring-tree* has a piece of flexible steel set into it at the waist. Bands of *webbing* are stretched on to the framework to carry the stuffing and leather finish.

The *stuffing* may be of wool, felt or foam rubber, and the underside of the saddle should be sufficiently stuffed to create a gullet

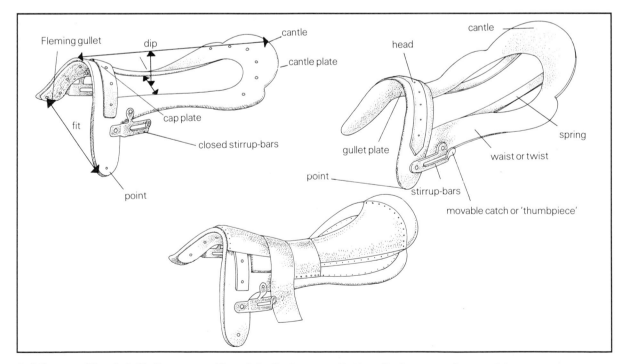

Saddle trees. **Top left** Ordinary tree. **Top right** Spring-tree. **Bottom** Spring-tree after straining.

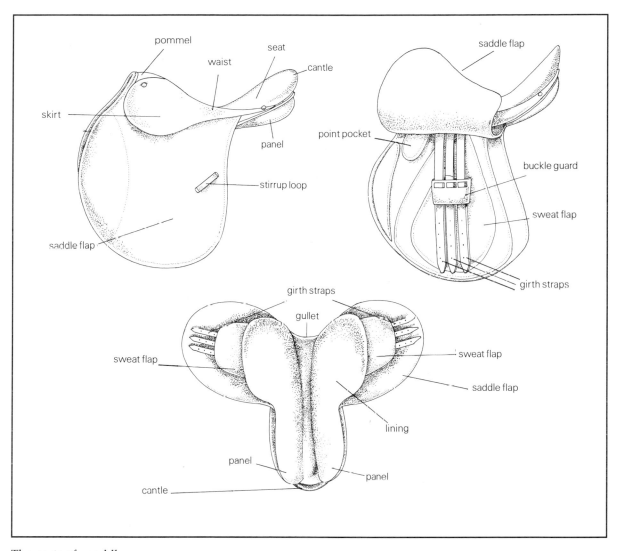

The parts of a saddle.

from the front to the back of the saddle and to give clearance over the pony's spine. Enough stuffing should be used on the seat to make the saddle comfortable for the rider.

Linings and leather panels and coverings are used to give the saddle its final familiar appearance.

There are three kinds of lining: linen, which is easy to clean, quick to dry and reasonably hard-wearing; serge, which is very absorbent, but wears quite quickly and is hard to clean; and leather, which cleans easily and lasts well, provided it is properly looked after.

The *panels* are the parts of the saddle closest to the horse. They carry the stuffing and lining. On a general-purpose saddle, the panels may have a roll of stuffing along each forward edge. These are known as knee-rolls,

and are designed to give support to the rider's knees. There are two types: full panel and half panel. The first reaches to the bottom of the saddle flap, the second only half-way down. The *girth straps* rest on the panel, although in some saddles there is an additional piece of leather, called a *sweat flap*, which lies between the panel and the girth straps. Most saddles are fitted with three girth straps, although the girth has only two buckles. You should alternate the straps you use in order to keep the wear on the saddle even.

The outer panel of the saddle is called the *saddle flap* and it should hang down far enough to hide the ends of the girth straps. The small flap of leather which conceals the stirrup-bars is known as the *skirt*.

The metal *stirrup-bars* are attached to the tree. They are usually fitted with safety-catches, small hinged ends which can be raised or lowered. You should always ride with the catches in the down position, so that the stirrup-leathers will come off if you happen to fall and your foot is trapped in the stirrup. The catches are put up *only* when you are carrying the saddle.

Always use a pair of *buckle guards* when riding to protect the saddle flaps and panels from being damaged by the girth buckles.

Fitting a saddle

If you are buying a new saddle for your pony, the wisest plan is to try it on the pony in the presence of a qualified saddler, who will be able to advise you on whether any small adjustments can be made by altering the stuffing, or whether you should try a different saddle altogether. However, if you don't have an expert to advise you, remember the following points.

The saddle is designed to distribute the rider's weight over the muscular parts of the horse's back. A saddle which is too long may throw the rider's weight back on to the loins. If it is too forward cut, there may be too much weight on the front of the saddle, which could eventually lead to soreness; and it may impede the pony's movements.

There should be no weight on the spine; daylight should be visible from front to back along the gullet when you are mounted. Check also that the gullet is wide enough to prevent any pressure along the edges of the spine.

The front arch of the saddle must be high enough and wide enough to prevent any pinching of the horse's withers. Some horses have high withers and need a saddle with a high, narrow arch. The waist of the saddle should be fairly narrow and the seat should be deep. This will help to bring the rider into the correct position.

Check the stirrup-bars; when you are mounted they should be horizontal and parallel to the ground. The stirrup-leathers, which are attached to the bars, will then hang perpendicular to the ground and your legs will be in the right place.

A pony's conformation may create problems when it comes to fitting a saddle. On a pony with a high wither the saddle may slip back, and a breastplate could be needed to keep it in place. On a small pony, with a low,

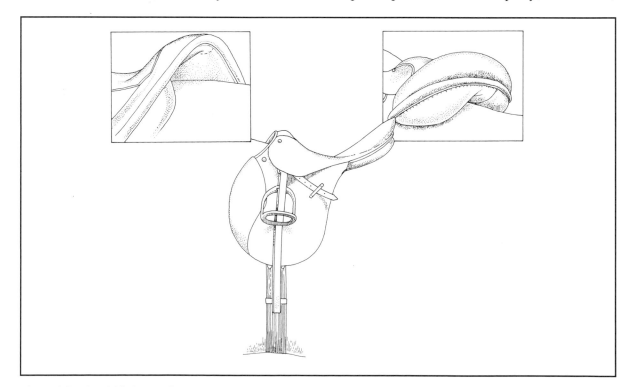

The saddle should fit properly, with adequate clearance over the spine. **Top Left** There should be no pressure on the withers by the front arch. **Top right** Daylight should be visible through the channel along the pony's spine.

flat wither, the saddle can slip forwards, and you would need a crupper to prevent this from happening.

Girths

Girths may be made of nylon, webbing, leather or lampwick.

Nylon girths are usually of single strands, linked at intervals by woven string and fitted with two buckles at each end. They are good general-purpose girths which grip well, especially on an unclipped pony. They can be washed easily and dry quickly.

Webbing girths are made of a single straight piece of webbing with one buckle at either end. They are inexpensive but can break. Two webbing girths should always be used together, one overlapping the other. Unless they are well looked after, they can get stiff with sweat and cause chafing.

Leather girths are hard-wearing but must be cared for properly if they are to stay soft and supple. There are three popular types. The Balding is divided into three along the centre portion. These three strips are then crossed over one another and stitched in place. The effect is to make the girth narrower at the places where it passes behind the horse's forelegs. The Atherstone is cut to a shape similar to the Balding, but it is one piece. To reinforce it, a strip of leather is sewn along its length. The Three-fold consists of a wide piece of leather folded into three. All these girths are fitted with two buckles at each end. The stitching on leather girths should always be carefully checked.

The *Lampwick* is a very soft girth of tubular, stocking-like material which stretches during use but goes back into shape afterwards. It has an inner lining of leather or webbing. It is fitted with two buckles at either end.

The *Cottage Craft* girth has become extremely popular in recent years. It is a straight girth of padded nylon material, reinforced with nylon webbing. Its advantages are that it can be easily washed and dried, and it does not chafe. It comes in a variety of colours and each end has two buckles.

Stirrup-leathers

These are made from ordinary leather, rawhide or buffalo hide. The latter two are very hard-wearing and largely unbreakable but are thicker than ordinary leather. Buffalo hide in particular stretches easily. Leathers should always be well cared for and the stitching checked regularly.

Stirrup-irons

They should be the right size for the rider, that is, about 2.5 cm (1 in) wider than the widest part of the boot. If they are too small, the foot could get caught in the stirrup; too big, and the rider's foot could slip right through. They should be of good quality metal, preferably stainless steel. With plated metal, the plating can chip or flake off. Solid

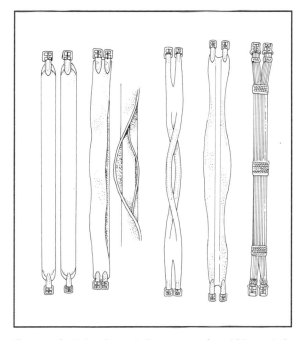

Types of girth, **from left**: a pair of webbing girths, Three-fold girth, Balding, Atherstone, nylon or string.

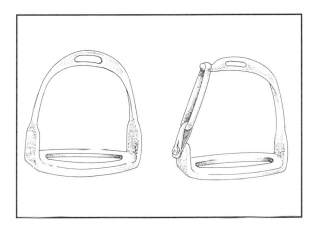

Stirrup-irons. **Left** Plain iron, and **right** safety iron.

nickel is too soft and brittle to be safe. The shape of the stirrup-iron is up to the rider and there are various styles on the market, but the standard iron is quite satisfactory. Safety stirrups have a rubber band instead of one metal side; it comes undone if, for any reason, the foot gets jammed in the stirrup. The drawback to these stirrups is that the rubber tends to become less elastic with use and the band can slip off unintentionally.

Pad saddles

With a first pony, particularly one which is small and round, a pad saddle is perfectly acceptable as a starting saddle. These saddles are made of felt, sometimes trimmed with leather, and have either no tree at all or just a part-tree forming a wither arch. The latter is better because it helps to keep the saddle in the right position. Pad saddles usually have their own webbing girth stitched to one side, which fastens by means of two buckles on the other side. If the saddle has a part-tree, it is usually fitted with proper stirrup-bars, but pad saddles with no tree may have D-rings instead of bars. These fittings should only be used with safety stirrups.

BUYING TACK

Always buy the best quality saddlery that you can afford. Bits are made from the same metal as stirrup-irons and the same standards apply to both. Stainless steel, hand-forged, is the best but it is also the most expensive.

Beware of some types of Asian saddles and bridles. The former may look perfectly all right, but inferior materials and workmanship in the parts of the saddle you cannot see could make the saddle dangerous. A second-hand English or German saddle is better value for money than a brand-new Asian import.

Some bridles, especially cheap ones, are made of Asian leather. Like the saddle, these may seem a good buy, but they tend to stretch with use, and quite noticeably when wet, which makes them dangerous.

Quite recently, bridles made from nylon webbing have been introduced. They are extremely practical for everyday use, but are not yet accepted in the show-ring. They are easy to care for because they can be washed. They can even be put in the washing-machine.

HEADCOLLAR AND LEAD-ROPE

A headcollar may be made of leather or nylon webbing, but in both cases the shape is the same. It consists of a noseband, held in place by a headpiece, with a section that passes under the cheek-bones and is linked to the noseband by a short strap. Wherever there is

Headcollar.

an intersection, a square or circular ring is used.

The nylon webbing headcollars are cheap and hard-wearing, and are the best buy for ponies, especially if your pony is difficult to catch and has to wear a headcollar while he is in the field. Leather headcollars look smart but they require much more care than the others and, of course, they are quite expensive.

Lead-ropes are made of jute or nylon, usually fitted with a clip so that it can be quickly fixed to the back of the headcollar. The cheapest lead-rope has a loop at one end, through which the free end of the rope passes after it has been put through the headcollar ring. The disadvantage of this method of fastening is that it can be very difficult to undo, especially if the rope is wet.

TACK CLEANING KIT

Your saddle and bridle will be safer and last much longer if you clean them properly. Few people manage to clean their tack *every* time they ride, but you should try to carry out this, for some reason most unwelcome, task at least once a week.

You will need a glycerine-based *saddle soap*, which comes in block form or in a tin, several sponges, a blunt knife and some leather oil. A few old matchsticks for removing saddle soap from buckle holes are useful.

Take both saddle and bridle apart and wash the bit and stirrup-irons in warm water. Wash the girth, unless it is made of leather, using a small nail-brush to remove the worst dirt, and hang it up to dry. Excess moisture should be removed with a towel. If you have a leather girth, clean it in the same way as the saddle.

Use the blunt knife to scrape off dried mud and the small blobs of grease, known as 'jockeys', which form on the lining of the saddle, the inside of the bridle and the end of the stirrup-leathers. A small, screwed-up pad of horse-hair is also effective at removing the 'jockeys'. With a damp sponge, well squeezed out, apply saddle soap to all leather surfaces, rubbing the soap in well. If the sponge is too wet, the soap will foam, which is good for cleaning but does not preserve the leather.

Once a month, apply a coating of leather oil to the tack after you have cleaned it, using a small brush, such as a soft paintbrush. The same oil should be put on any leather items of tack you are intending to store. It will keep the leather supple and prevent it from cracking.

The bit and stirrup-irons should be dried and buffed with a soft cloth, if they are stainless steel. Any other metal will need shining with metal polish, but polish should not be used on stainless steel as it dulls it.

Reassemble the saddle and bridle and put them carefully away.

SADDLE AND BRIDLE RACKS

It is possible to buy special racks for saddles and bridles, which can be put up in a cupboard, utility room or dry shed. They are specially designed to carry the tack without causing any damage. If you cannot afford to buy them ready-made, it is possible to make them.

Saddle put up on a home-made rack.

A saddle rack should be shaped so that the saddle rests on its stuffing and not on the gullet. If you do have to put the saddle on the ground, stand it on the pommel, with the cantle leaning against the wall, protected from damage by the girth or a piece of cloth.

A piece of wood, cut from a log, or an old

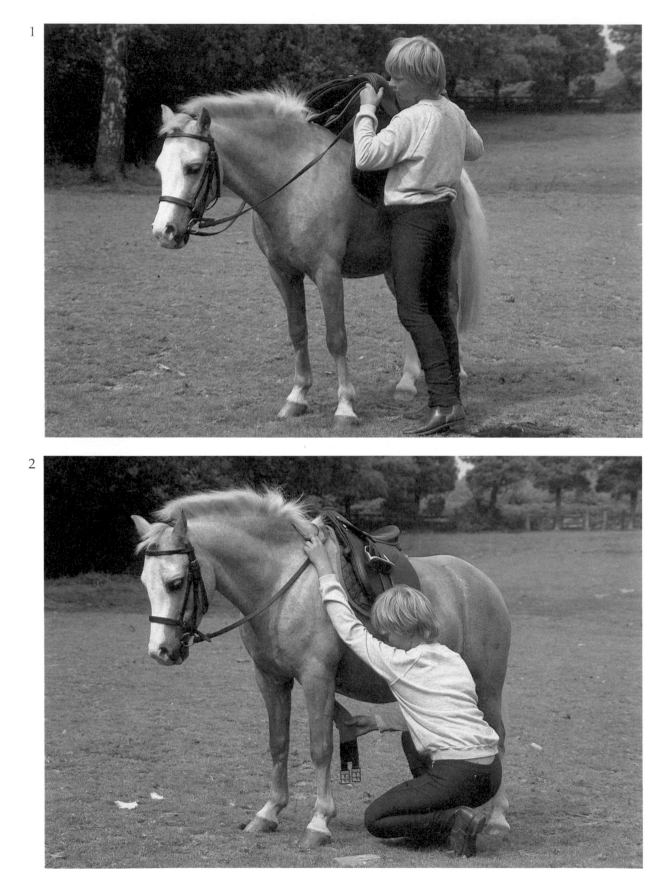

3

4

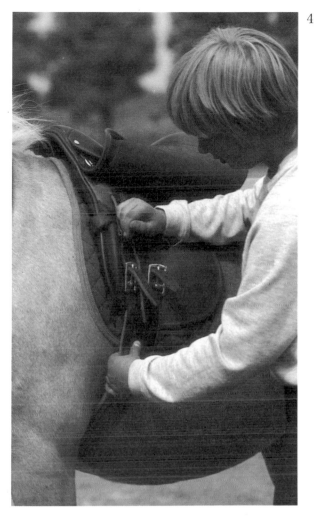

Saddling up. **1** Place the saddle in position on the pony's back, whilst keeping hold of the reins so that the pony does not move off. The saddle should be put well up on the withers and then slid back into the correct place. This ensures that the hairs underneath are lying the right way. **2** Bring the girth under the pony's belly from the offside to the near side. One hand still restrains the pony from moving off. **3** Doing up the girth buckles. This is the point at which a ticklish pony may get restive or put his ears back. Another awkward trick which many ponies adopt is to blow out their tummies so that it is difficult to get the buckles done up. If your pony does this, remember to tighten the girths a few minutes later when he has forgotten the trick. **4** Always run your hand down the inside of the girth to see that the hairs are lying straight and that no folds of skin are being pinched.

A saddle horse. Never store saddles on top of one another.

saddle soap tin screwed to the wall, are just the right shape for a bridle hook. Never hang your bridle on a coat hook or a nail – the weight of the bridle causes the leather to bend too sharply and eventually it can crack and break.

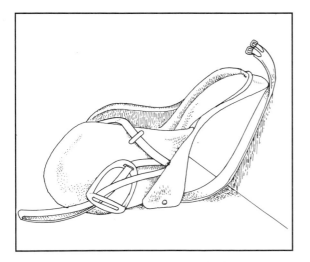

When a saddle is put on the ground, place it as shown, using the girth to protect the pommel and cantle.

GROOMING KIT

You can build up a grooming kit gradually or buy the items all in one go. Either way, you will need a box or bag to keep them in; preferably a light-weight box which is easy to carry. Some items are more important than others, so if you are planning to buy things gradually you should follow the order given here.

Hoof-pick This should be at the top of everyone's list because a pony's feet are so important. You use the hoof-pick to clean out the mud and small stones which collect in the sole and crevices of the hoof. The hooves should be picked out daily.

Body brush This is a soft, short-bristled brush which is used to remove dust and scurf from the coat and on the mane and tail.

Curry-comb A rubber curry-comb is useful for removing caked mud from the coat of a grass-kept pony. A metal curry-comb cleans the body brush.

Stable sponges These are ordinary foam rubber sponges used for cleaning the eyes, nose, muzzle and dock.

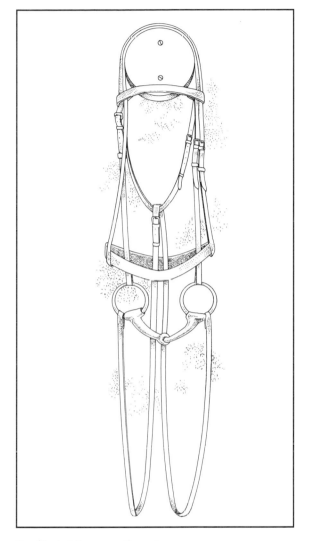

Snaffle bridle correctly put up.

Dandy-brush This is a coarse-bristled brush which can be used on a grass-kept pony to remove mud, dust and heavy dirt. It should not be used on the head or on the bony areas of the legs.

Water brush This has thick, soft bristles and is used to dampen the mane and tail when plaiting and to remove stains from the coat of a stable-kept horse.

Mane comb This is a broad, flat comb, made of metal or plastic, which is useful for dividing the mane when plaiting or in assisting with the pulling of hairs at the top of the

tail. The object of the latter is to give the top of the tail a neat, tidy appearance, but it should never be carried out on a pony at grass because it deprives him of essential protection.

Hoof oil and brush The oil is applied to the outside of the hoof and the bulbs of the heels, to make the feet look smart and to help them if the horn is brittle or broken.

As you become more experienced, you will find yourself adding items to your grooming kit. A **stable-rubber**, for example, is like a big, linen tea-towel and it is used to give a final polish to a pony. An ordinary tea-towel is just as good as a cloth sold especially for the purpose. **Needles**, **plaiting bands** and **sewing thread** will be required when you have reached the stage of taking part in shows or of going hunting. A **sweat-scraper**, which is semi-circular in shape and has a rubber scraper attached, is used to remove sweat easily from a hot horse so that he will dry off quickly. It is also useful for removing shampoo or rinsing water from a pony which has been washed.

Shampoo This is another item which finds its way into most pony-owners' grooming kits. Special horse shampoos are available from saddlers and are better for your pony than your mother's expensively-scented shampoo from France. Washing-up liquid is very effective, as long as you remember to rinse it off thoroughly.

BUCKETS

You will need a number of buckets. One or two are just not enough. One bucket will be required to feed the pony from; another one or two will be needed for water. If you plan to feed sugar beet to your pony in the winter, you will want a bucket to soak it in. It is best to buy several inexpensive buckets, and immediately paint your name or your pony's name on them. This will prevent arguments if you are sharing the field with someone else's pony. All except the most expensive rubber buckets will deteriorate in time. They tend to become brittle when left outside in frosty weather, and ponies tread on them, kick them and sometimes even lie on them. All in all, a bucket has a rough life, so calculate the number you will need and add one more.

Pages 48–9 Bridling. **1** One hand holds the headpiece while the other gently guides the bit into the pony's mouth. **2** Once the bit is in, the headpiece is slid over the pony's ears. **3** The throat lash is brought to the nearside and **4** buckled. **5** Finally, the buckle of the cavesson noseband is fastened.

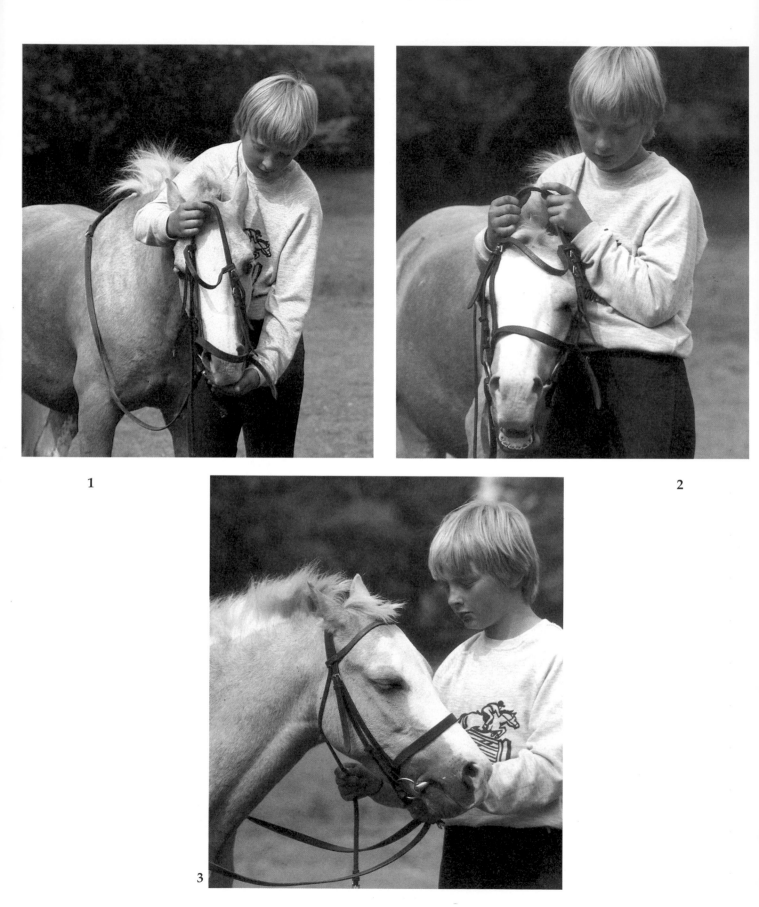

1

2

3

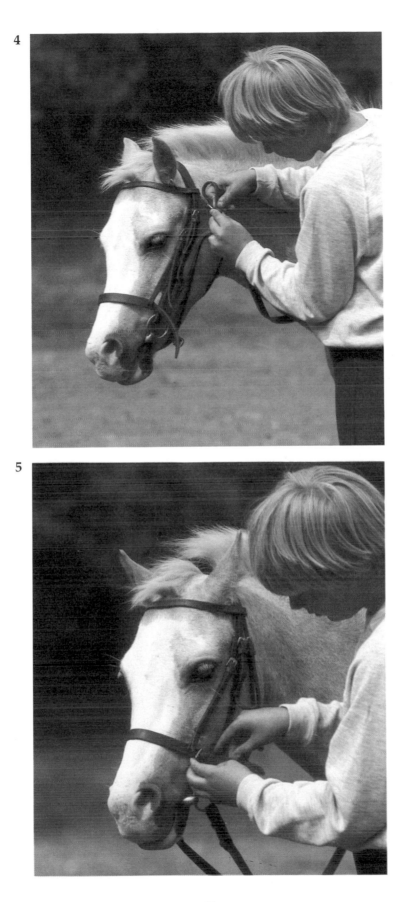

CHAPTER 5
Feeding and general care

Ponies do extremely well on a diet of grass. It is, after all, their natural food and they can cope quite comfortably with light work without any supplementary feeding of concentrates, such as oats or cubes. Summer grazing provides all the nutriments a pony needs; in winter, when there is little goodness in the grass, he should be given hay (grass which has been cut and dried at a time when its nutritional value is high).

A first pony is unlikely to be asked to do more work than a grass-only diet can sustain. This makes him reasonably inexpensive to keep. Although grass-fed ponies are healthy, they are not completely fit. They look bright-eyed and bouncy, but their fat is soft. Too much galloping will make them sweat and puff, but while you are still a novice your riding is unlikely to be too strenuous. It is only when your riding advances to the point that you want to enter for competitions, to ride a cross-country course, or to go out for a day's hunting, that your pony needs concentrated feed and a rigorous programme of exercise to build up his muscles and make him athletically fit.

The rules of feeding remain the same whether your pony is doing no more than a little light hacking, or hunting hard three or four days a week. It is the quantity and type of food which change.

A horse has a complicated digestive system, with a remarkably small stomach for his size. He needs to eat little and often, a programme which is easily maintained in the wild or when he is turned out into a field.

If you were to watch your pony throughout twenty-four hours, you would see that he spends long periods grazing, short periods resting, and that he intersperses these activities with an occasional burst of exercise, such as cantering around and bucking, and a few visits to the water trough.

A horse's digestive organs should always have some food in them, and grass or hay provides the necessary bulk.

First-time owners are often uncertain when to start giving a pony hay. In some countries, for example Britain, the winters can be very mild, and the cold weather may come early or late. It is difficult, therefore, to lay down a definite programme. The table opposite, however, offers guide-lines to the amounts which should be given daily.

The table does not take into account the short feeds which will help to see a hard-working grass-kept pony through the winter months. There are various types of grain—oats, barley, maize and so on—mixtures, cubes and other products, available from corn merchants, which will supplement the pony's winter hay ration. However, whichever you choose to give, and in what quantity, depends entirely on the amount of work your pony will be doing.

With a first pony and a novice rider, it is important to select the right ingredients for a short feed. Just because you have heard that oats are good for horses, do not assume that is what your pony must have. Some concentrates create energy and, unless your pony is able to work off that energy, you will be facing all sorts of problems. It is better to give your pony more hay than to introduce concentrates into his diet without taking expert advice.

	Size of pony		
	Under 12 hh	12 to 13 hh	13 to 14 hh
Early spring	2.2–3.2 kg (5–7 lb)	3.2–4.1 kg (7–9 lb)	4.1–5 kg (9–11 lb)
Late spring	No hay need be given unless your pony has a tendency to get very fat on grass. Then you should, if possible, put him in a stable for three to four hours with a small haynet.		
Summer	No hay	No hay	No hay
Early autumn	Start offering a small quantity of hay if the weather is cold or wet. If the hay is not eaten by the next day, leave for a week, then try again.		
Late autumn	Gradually increase the amount of hay.		
Winter	2.2–4.5 kg (5–10 lb)	4.5–5.4 kg (10–12 lb)	5.4–6.8 kg (12–15 lb)

A guide to the amount of hay that should be fed daily to a grass-kept pony.

HAY

There are several types of hay, depending on the pasture that it is made from. In the UK there are three types – seed, meadow and clover – of which the first two are the best for horses. In the USA, alfalfa hay is the most commonly available.

Seed hay is hay grown from selected seeds, usually such grasses as Cocksfoot, Timothy, Crested Dogs-tail, and Perennial and Italian Rye-grasses. Sometimes red and white clover is added. If it has been properly sown and cared for and harvested at the right time – between the flowering and seeding stages – it will be nutritious without being overheating.

Meadow hay comes from permanent meadows and should contain all or some of the grasses mentioned above. It may also contain perennial weeds such as docks, dandelions, buttercups and thistles. This does not matter very much as long as they do not make up the bulk of the contents. Like seed hay, it should have been harvested at the proper time and, when new, will be greenish in colour and soft to the touch. As it grows older, the colour fades.

Clover hay is dark in colour, rather brittle and very sweet-smelling. It is grown from seed-sown clovers and is extremely nutritious, particularly for cattle. However, it is too rich for horses and ponies, and should never be offered to ponies except in small quantities mixed with another type of hay.

Alfalfa is made from lucerne and is particularly common in the USA. It is a protein-rich food, much richer than meadow hay, and smaller quantities would be needed to keep a pony fit and well. Late-cut alfalfa can be woody, and a pony might take some time to get used to it. It is dustier than ordinary hay and needs to be sprinkled with water before being offered to horses. Cubes or pellets made from alfalfa are richer than hay is in vitamin A and calcium.

In addition, you may come across *Horsehage*, the proprietary name for a guaranteed dust-free form of dried grass, which is supplied vacuum-packaged in bags. It is ideal for horses which suffer from chronic respiratory problems or allergies to ordinary hay.

Good quality hay smells pleasant and is reasonably free from dust. If possible, hay should be between six and eighteen months old before being given to horses. This means that some of the previous season's crop should be saved to start off the following winter. As a general rule, hay taken from the field in mid-summer should not be fed to ponies until the following mid-winter. The reason for this is that new hay still has some chemical changes to go through while in store, before it becomes easy to digest.

Never buy hay which is yellow, blackish, wet or mouldy, and if, because your storage conditions are not very good, your hay has reached this state by the end of the winter, it is better to scrap the remaining bales and buy in some more.

When and where you buy your hay depends on the amount of storage space you have. A dry shed or barn with a concrete floor is the ideal place to store hay, and it will keep well if the stack stands on a layer of pallets. One pony will consume approximately one tonne (one ton) of hay during the winter. This is about fifty bales (each bale some 25.4 kg (56 lb), or quite a large stack. You are lucky indeed if you have room to store a whole winter's supply because it means that you can buy your hay 'off the field', which is usually the cheapest way of buying it. Buying off the field means that you arrange with a local farmer to take the amount of hay you think you will need straight from the field where it is being harvested. You may have to collect it yourself, or for a small extra fee the farmer might deliver the load to you. His willingness to do this depends on how advanced he is with the harvest, and on the weather. If he still has several fields to tackle, he may say that he cannot spare the time.

The collection of hay from the field is not a job that can be postponed. If the opportunity of buying the hay comes along on a Monday or Tuesday, it is very risky to wait until the following weekend. The fine weather may break, and heavy rain will ruin the hay. Better to miss a ride or the chance to go swimming, and set off there and then. Persuade your parents to make several journeys with the car, if necessary, or borrow a small lorry or a horse-trailer. A trailer, incidentally, can carry between thirty and forty bales, but you will need as many strong people to help you as you can muster.

If you do not have enough storage space to buy hay in bulk, you will have to buy hay as you need it. Most people can find the space to store six or eight bales at a time and this represents about two weeks supply for your pony. If you can find a supplier who will sell you enough for the winter but allow you to pick up the hay when you need it, you will probably not have to pay very much more per bale than buying 'off the field'. However, if you have to buy hay in very small quantities, you will find that the price tends to rise as the winter goes on, and especially if the spring is wet or prolonged and hay supplies become hard to get. Bought this way, it can also vary considerably in quality.

Never forget that hay is the most important winter food that you can give your pony. Try to get good quality hay, and do not be mean in the amount you give. Avoid 'bargain offers', especially at the end of the winter. If hay is advertised at a suspiciously cheap price, the likelihood is that it has deteriorated while in store; perhaps it was not properly dried, and much of it will not only be unfit to eat, but could be harmful. A hungry pony will eat poor hay but it will do him little good.

THE DAILY FEEDING ROUTINE: WINTER

Ponies should be given hay at the same time each day. No doubt the best time is straight after school and before it has grown dark. You can provide the hay in a haynet or put it straight on the ground. There are advantages and drawbacks to both methods.

A haynet is the least wasteful. You simply stuff the net full of hay, pull the drawstring tight and tie it to a convenient fence-rail or post or to a tree. This method keeps the hay clear of mud, and very little will be trampled underfoot. However, you must make absolutely certain that the net is tied high enough to clear the ground even when it is half-empty, and an empty haynet hangs much lower than a full one. Unless its anchoring point is really secure – such as a tree – the tugging of the pony as he pulls out each mouthful can put a strain on the post or rail, which may eventually loosen it. You can then end up with an insecure fence. The haynet should always be tied with a quick-release knot.

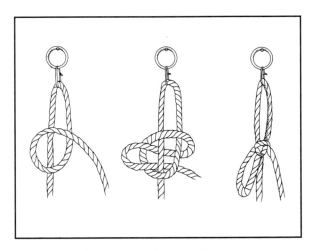

The stages of tying a quick-release knot.

Opposite Always use a body brush on a pony's head, forelock and around his ears.

Hay placed on the ground is the most natural method for a pony to feed. However, some of the hay will be wasted, especially if the ground is wet or poached. This is probably the best method if there are several ponies in the field. Place the hay in piles well apart from one another to keep quarrelling to a minimum, and always add an extra pile to

give shy ponies the chance to eat their fill. Bossy ponies seem to delight in moving from one pile to another, forcing the others to move on.

Ponies soon learn when to expect your arrival with their food and will be waiting for you. If you are late, they will get restless and may start kicking and biting. So work out a routine that fits into the rest of your activities and stick to it.

A visit once a day is usually sufficient. If the weather is frosty or there is snow on the ground, you should go twice. A small feed of hay on frosty mornings is beneficial. In any case, you should visit the field early to break the ice on the water trough. During long spells of icy weather, you may have to bring fresh water to the field in buckets. At this time of the year, it is particularly important to keep the trough well filled – each time you remove chunks of ice, you are lowering the water level, and if the hose or pipe which supplies the water is exposed, it can freeze solid.

During your visit to the field, always check your pony over carefully. Look particularly at his feet. On hard, frozen ground, an unshod pony's hooves may crack or split or he may suffer from a bruised sole or heels. There is less chance of any of these problems happening if the pony is shod. When there is snow on the ground, the snow can collect in the foot and form a hard ball of ice, a common reason for bruising. The best way of ensuring that the snow does not collect is to smear the sole of the foot with motor grease.

When the weather is wet, the ground will get soggy and poached. Watch out for cracked heels or mud fever, which are both due to an infection contracted by getting the legs and feet caked with mud. The symptoms are sore patches on the legs and belly or deep cracks in the heels. The infection can be prevented by smearing petroleum jelly around the heels and over the pastern and fetlock joint. Ponies, with plenty of hair on the legs and around the fetlocks, are less likely to suffer from the condition than horses.

THE DAILY FEEDING ROUTINE: SUMMER

Even though you are not feeding your pony in summer, you should visit him every day. As the evenings grow lighter you will be able to ride him more often. Remember, however, that he is in soft condition, so do not gallop him about too much. Always return from a ride quietly, giving him a chance to cool down before you turn him out into the field.

Keep his water trough clean. In hot weather, algae can form very quickly, turning the water green and slimy. The trough will need a once-a-week scrubbing and hosing out, before being refilled with fresh water.

Flies can be a problem, particularly at dusk. Shade is very necessary to ponies. Use a proprietary fly-repellent on the face and body. A fly fringe, which fits on to the headcollar like a browband, is good at keeping flies away from the pony's eyes. A gauze fly-mask which fits over his ears and fastens under the cheek-bones is also effective, and ponies rarely object to wearing them.

GROOMING

The purpose of grooming is to stimulate the skin, to remove mud and loose hairs from the coat, and to make the pony look clean and tidy. There is no need to groom the pony if you are not intending to ride him, and you should never be too vigorous in your attentions to a pony which lives out.

The reason for this is that the pony's coat is his principal means of keeping warm and dry. When you run your hand through a pony's coat, you will notice a greasy deposit on your fingers. The same greasy deposit gets on the tack and on your boots. This is a natural grease which helps to keep your pony waterproof. A pony's winter coat is made up of short, thick hairs covered by a thatch of longer hairs. The short, thick hairs provide insulation, the longer ones repel rain-water. In dry, cold weather, the pony looks like a shaggy bear, quite different from the shiny, sleek creature of the summer months. His coat is well designed to keep out the worst of the weather. Even his mane and tail take on a bushy look.

In winter, therefore, confine your grooming simply to removing caked-on mud, and the tangles from his mane and tail. The best tools for this purpose are a rubber curry-comb or stiff-bristled dandy-brush for the mud, and the body brush for the mane and tail. Use a hoof-pick to clean out the underside of his hooves. The hoof-pick, in fact, is the only item you should use every day.

In spring, your pony will start to lose his winter coat. This is a very tedious time of the

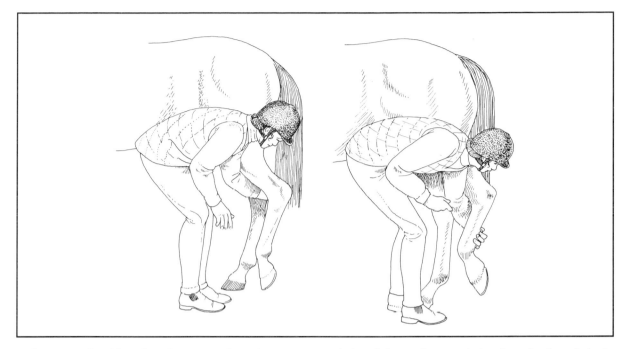

Picking up a hind leg. Stand to one side and run your inside hand down the pony's leg from hock to fetlock. Grasp the fetlock and gently pull the foot upwards.

year both for him and you, as the process of losing his coat will make him feel itchy and will cover you, whenever you ride, with quantities of loose hairs. You can help to speed the transition from winter to summer coat by grooming him regularly, making a big effort to get rid of the clumps of matted loose hair which tend to form on his chest and belly and between his legs.

Gradually, however, the summer coat emerges. Now the woolly bear resembles a pony once again. The summer coat is short and has a healthy sheen. There will still be a layer of grease on the pony's skin, necessary to protect him against summer rain, and you may well raise a cloud of dust when you pat the pony. Any loose bits of grass and surface dust should be removed with the body brush, and on smart occasions, a going-over with a dampened water brush will help to stop the dust from flying about. Now is the time to trim the hair from his fetlocks – it will grow again in readiness for the winter. Always remember to clean out his feet and use damp sponges to wipe his eyes, nostrils, muzzle and dock.

At the end of the summer, the winter coat starts to grow. The first signs are a loosening of the short hairs and the disappearance of

the sheen. Gradually, you become aware that the pony is taking on a furry look once more. Now you should be more careful than ever not to remove too much grease when you groom.

CARE OF THE FEET

Very few people nowadays are able to take their ponies to the forge and most rely on the farrier visiting them. Farriers travel round with the necessary equipment: portable anvils, a collection of shoes and nails, and sometimes even a portable brazier.

If the farrier brings his own fire, or you can call at a forge, your pony can be hot-shod in the traditional way. This means that the farrier can hold the hot shoe to the pony's foot and make any necessary adjustments to its size and shape.

Cold-shoeing, provided it is carried out by a farrier who knows his job, is perfectly satisfactory. If it is the first time the farrier has shod your pony, ask him to look at the pony's feet and take the measurements himself. He will then make the shoes at his forge and return to put them on. If he asks you to give him details of the shoe sizes, you should measure across the widest part of the pony's existing shoes and again from heel to toe.

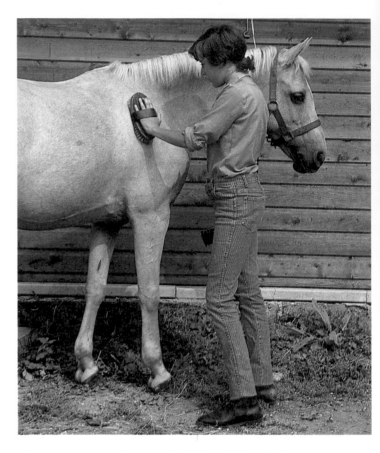

Above Grooming the nearside **left**, and the offside **right**. Note that you always use the right hand on the near side, and the left hand on the offside, regardless of whether you are right-handed or left-handed.

Left Grooming the tail. Use a body brush, and brush a small section at a time.

Below Remember to sponge the nostrils, and around the mouth and eyes.

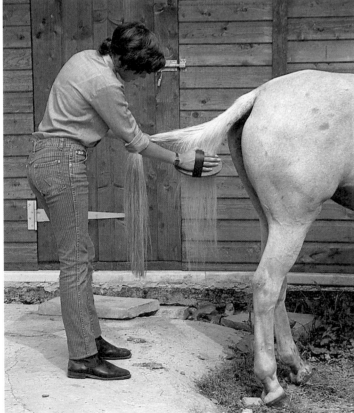

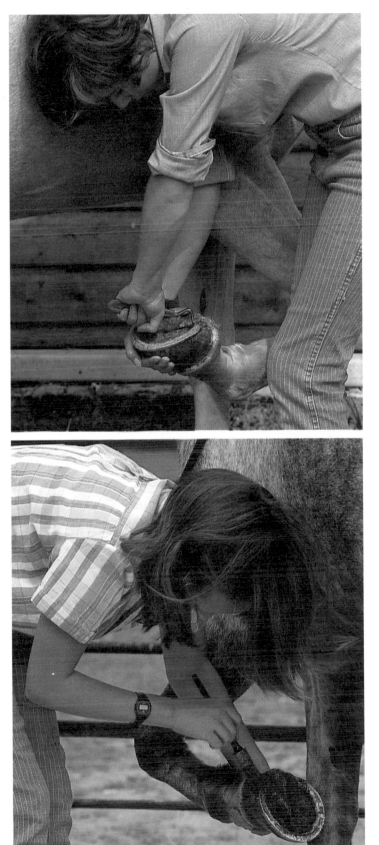

Above Picking out the front and hind hooves.
Always stand close to the pony's body, and hold the
hoof in the inside hand.

Left and below To smarten up your pony's feet for a
show or special occasion, you can oil the heels and the
walls of the hooves. Use a soft brush and apply the oil
liberally. Never kneel on the ground beside a pony's
feet; crouch beside him, so that you can move out of
the way quickly if he stamps his foot or kicks out.

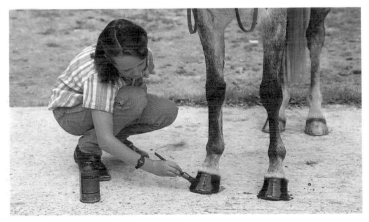

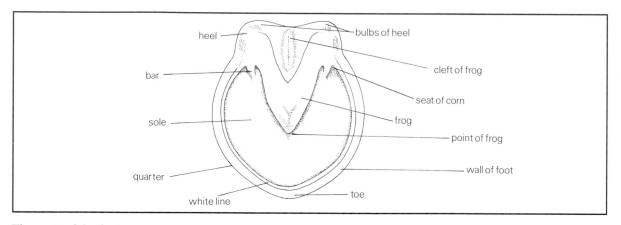

The parts of the foot.

After the first shoeing, the farrier will keep a record of your pony's requirements.

Most farriers charge at a rate of so much per set of shoes, plus travelling expenses and VAT. Where more than one pony is to be shod, travelling expenses can be shared. Because a pony's feet are so important, it is better to pay more for the services of a really reputable farrier than risk ruining your pony's feet by going to a cut-price, incompetent one.

Some ponies are heavier on their shoes than others, and only experience will tell you how often your pony needs shoeing. Examine the shoes each time you pick out the pony's feet. Examine the clenches: the part of the nail that emerges through the wall of the hoof, is twisted off and hammered down. As the shoes wear, the clenches may rise. As the hoof grows, it may overgrow the shoe. In time, parts of the shoe wear thin, and sometimes a shoe works loose. You should always be on the look-out for tell-tale signs and be ready to make your appointment with the farrier.

His first task is to remove the old shoes. This he does by hammering up the clenches and levering the shoe off with a pair of pincers. He will then trim away the overgrown horn, levelling the foot so that, even when the shoe is in place, the frog, which absorbs jar and helps to stop the pony from slipping, will come in contact with the ground. He tests the new shoe against the foot and

may make a few minor adjustments to it, using his hammer and anvil.

Once satisfied, he fixes the shoe in place with nails. Herein lies much of the skill of the farrier. The wall of the hoof is insensitive, and it will not hurt the pony to have nails driven into this part. The point of each nail emerges higher up on the outside of the hoof. If the farrier is careless, he can place the nail too close to the sensitive inside of the sole, which will quickly cause lameness, or too close to the outside, which will cause part of the hoof to break away and the shoe to be loosened.

When all the nails (usually seven) are hammered home, the farrier twists off their points and hammers over the ends, or clenches. Finally, he rasps the horn smooth.

Ponies who do little roadwork may not need new shoes each time the farrier calls. Unless the shoes are badly worn, he may decide to trim the feet and replace the old shoes. These are known as removes and the charge is less than for supplying new shoes. Be guided by your farrier's advice, and if your pony has any problems with his feet talk them over with him. Special shoes may, in some cases, counteract the effects of poor conformation or clumsy leg action.

It is difficult to be definite about how often your pony should need shoeing. A visit from the farrier may be necessary at intervals of anything from four weeks to three months, depending on how much work the pony has to do and how quickly his feet grow.

CHAPTER 6
Clothing for rider and pony

Riding clothes are designed to be practical and smart, but above all to give the rider protection in the event of an accident. Most people know that, for safety's sake, they should always wear a proper riding hat. But did you know that it is just as important to wear the correct type of shoes or boots?

THE RIDER'S CLOTHING

Safety and comfort are the two most important elements in the choice of riding clothes.

Hats

It may surprise many people to know that riding is one of the most dangerous of all sports: in Britain, for example, it has the highest number of fatalities per year. And of all injuries sustained in riding accidents, around two-thirds are suffered by the head.

A hard hat, therefore, is essential. It should be made to a standard approved by the national body governing safety standards. (In the UK this is the British Standards Institution, and their approved products bear a label with the well-known BSI 'kite' mark.)

In 1984, the BSI, together with manufacturers and leading members of the horse world, met together to produce a riding hat with a higher degree of safety than before. The result was the new British Standard No 6473, which replaced the old BS 3686.

The new standard means that the hat has a greater resistance to impact than before and that it must be so fitted that it will stay in place at all times.

To achieve this, it has a high-quality shell, flexible peak, impact-absorbing ventilation button, and a urethane shell liner and self-conforming head pad replacing the drawstring system. The old drawstring, which should always have been pulled tight enough to leave a cushion of air between the top of the hat and the head, was far too often left undone or was so slackly tied that it was useless. In the new hat, the shock-absorbing head pad is built in.

Finally, the hat has a specially developed three point harness which can be used with or without a chin cup.

In appearance, the hat is little different from earlier hats. It is velvet-covered and available in various colours. Most people prefer black, navy blue or dark brown. As before, it is trimmed with a ribbon bow at the back, but unless you are the child of a farmer or a hunt servant, you should cut off the ribbons or fold them under and stitch them down.

Since 1986, every competitor in Pony Club competitions has had to wear a jockey skull cap, BS4472. However, the Pony Club will now accept BS6473, *provided that* fixed inside it is a label stating: 'This hat meets with the impact (or performance) requirements of BS4472'.

You may already possess a suitable skull-cap, especially if you enter cross-country events and hunter trials. The skull-cap – or crash cap – has a glass fibre shell, and lightweight silk covers in different colours can be bought for it. It is held on by means of a chin harness. You should always take trouble to buy a crash hat that fits you properly, and a well-fitting hat is not uncomfortable.

If you have a bad fall, or your hat receives a blow or kick, you should have the hat examined by an expert before continuing to use it. A damaged hat *must* be replaced.

Boots

Whatever type of footwear you choose, it must have a clearly defined heel. The heel prevents your foot from slipping through the stirrup-iron and perhaps getting jammed if you fall. For this reason flat-soled shoes, such as gymshoes and trainers, are dangerous for riding. Wellington boots are also unsuitable because they are wider than riding boots would be, and may get caught in the stirrup-iron.

For young children, jodhpur boots are sensible, comfortable and hard-wearing. They protect the ankle from being rubbed by the stirrup-iron, and they have a proper heel. They are usually black or brown and have either an elasticated gusset or a strap and buckle fastening.

Rubber, knee-length riding boots are a recent innovation and can be worn over jodhpurs or with conventional breeches. They are shaped to the leg and the top is cut away slightly on the inside. They are easy to keep clean because mud and grease can be sponged off. Before buying a pair, however, try them not only for foot comfort but also for length. Some are quite high and can cut into the back of the knee when the leg is bent.

They are not a substitute for wellington boots because the sole is not grooved and gives little grip when you are walking in mud.

Jodhpurs

A pair of stretch jodhpurs are comfortable and practical, and they wash easily. If made from two-way stretch material, they give complete freedom of movement. Most riders have more than one pair, keeping light-coloured ones (white, yellow, cream or fawn) for important occasions and using dark-coloured ones (dark brown or dark green) for everyday use. Stretch denim jodhpurs are also popular for general wear.

Always try on jodhpurs before you buy them as, to be effective, the strappings must be in the right place. The strappings are those extra pieces which line the inside of the knee and half-way down the calf, preventing chafing or pinching from the stirrup-leathers. On very expensive jodhpurs and breeches, the strappings are made of soft suede, but this means that they have to be dry-cleaned.

Ordinary denim jeans or cotton trousers can be used for casual riding, but they give less protection to the inside of the leg.

Jackets

A riding jacket is slightly waisted, and has a flared skirt and one or two slits at the back. The shape ensures that it hangs properly and looks smart when the wearer is in the saddle. For young children, a tweed jacket is suitable for all occasions. However, later on, if you enter showing classes, you will need a black, brown or navy blue showing jacket as well. Showing jackets usually have a velvet collar. In jumping classes at a show, even on a hot day, the judge will often insist on your wearing a jacket. This is because it provides some protection for your arms, shoulders and back should you be unlucky enough to fall off.

For everyday riding, there is no need to wear a jacket as a sweat-shirt and anorak, or jersey and quilted waistcoat, are comfortable and practical.

Shirt and tie

These are necessary only when you are showing or jumping. The shirt should be a plain pale colour, such as white, blue, fawn or yellow, and the tie should also be plain coloured. A Pony Club tie, with its distinctive pale blue, gold and purple stripes, is always correct.

Gloves

String gloves, leather gloves, or gloves with leather palms will help you to grip the reins on a wet day. They are always part of a showing outfit whatever the weather. Gloves tend to get lost easily so it is wise to have a spare pair.

Hair

Hair should always be tidy. Long hair can be plaited in one or two plaits; medium-length or short hair needs a hairnet to keep it in place. Ear-rings should never be worn while riding, nor should other forms of jewelry except a Pony Club or similar badge.

THE PONY'S CLOTHING

If you look round a saddler's shop or flick through the advertising pages of a horse magazine, you could be forgiven for wondering whether your pony is an animal or a fashion model. There are all manner of rugs in many different materials, brightly-coloured bandages, items in felt, leather and rubber to protect the pony's legs, waterproof sheets to

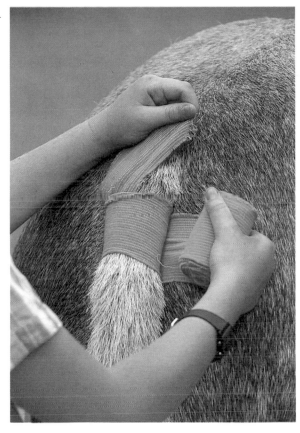

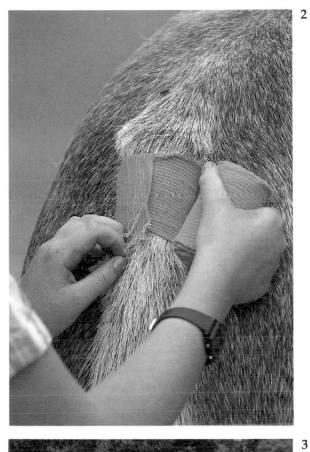

Putting on a tail bandage. **1** Start by holding the end against the top of the tail and take a turn round the tail to keep the end in position. **2** Fold over the projecting end and carry on winding, down to the end of the dock and back up again. **3** Finish off by tying the tapes round the tail, neatly and securely but not too tightly.

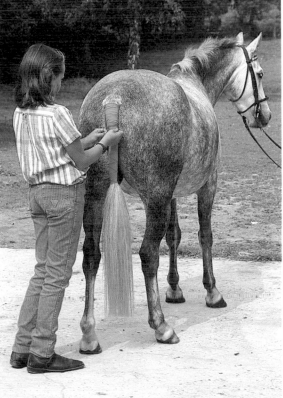

keep off the rain, furry numnahs to go under the saddle, and so on.

None of these things is necessary for a novice rider with a grass-kept pony. Nature has given him a perfectly adequate fur rug of his own, which has all the necessary warmth-giving and waterproofing qualities. Provided he can exercise himself properly and has plenty of fresh water and food, he can cope with all forms of weather and remain bright-eyed and healthy.

Remember that all native breeds of pony are hardy and tough by nature. What such a pony does *not* need is a New Zealand rug, and you should resist the temptation to buy him one. A New Zealand rug is an outdoor rug designed to keep a *clipped* horse warm and dry when he is running loose in a field. It is cut to a special shape and fitted with straps and sometimes a surcingle, in order that it will stay in place even when the horse rolls.

Unfortunately, many pony-owners believe that an unclipped pony also needs a New Zealand rug. In consequence, at the first sign of bad weather in the autumn, the poor pony is bundled into his winter clothing and has to suffer the discomfort of wearing it for the next six months. Yet the disadvantages of such a rug on a pony with a full winter coat are numerous.

First of all, it flattens the coat, reducing its natural insulation. Secondly, it tends to impede the pony's movements, making it more difficult for him to move about in order to keep warm. Thirdly, on mild days, it can make the pony too hot, so that he starts to sweat. As the sweat cools, his body gets clammy and he can easily catch cold.

A New Zealand rug, even if it fits well, can chafe, particularly on the points of the shoulders and over the withers. The leg straps, where they pass between the hind legs, may also rub. At least twice a day, the pony must be caught and the rug checked to see that it has not slipped.

Far better, therefore, to leave your pony with his own natural coat.

Tail bandage

This is likely to be the only item of clothing a first pony will need. You use it to make the hairs at the top of the tail stay in place. It is also part of the protective clothing that a pony wears when he is travelling. A tail bandage is made of stockinette or crepe and is rolled up from the tape end, with the sewn side of the tape inwards.

To put on a tail bandage, start by dampening the top of the tail slightly with the water brush. Unroll about 25 cm (10 in) of the bandage; pass this underneath the tail as high up as it will go. Hold the free end firmly in place at the root of the tail with one hand; with the other hand, unroll the bandage over the free end, and then make one complete turn of the tail. Fold down the loose end and take a turn over it and round the tail, slightly higher than the first turn. Continue to unroll the bandage round the tail, moving downwards and overlapping the turns as you go. Stop just short of the end of the tail bone and tie the tapes securely, but not too tightly.

Never wet the bandage before you put it on, in case it shrinks and injures the tail, nor leave a tail bandage on all night. If it is tight enough to stay in place for the whole night it is too tight, and could interfere with the circulation and harm the tail.

To remove a tail bandage, undo the tapes, then take hold of the bandage at the top of the tail and, using both hands, slide it downwards and off the tail in one quick movement.

CHAPTER 7
Shows and gymkhanas

Once you have a pony of your own, you will almost certainly want to take him to shows and gymkhanas. Competitions are fun and it is exciting to win rosettes to pin up on your bedroom wall.

HOW TO ENTER

The gymkhana season begins in the spring, and continues to the autumn. Apart from shows and gymkhanas, there are also hunter trials and one-day events, but if you are a beginner you should start off with small, local gymkhanas where the emphasis is very much on fun.

These events are usually advertised in the local papers or by means of posters put up in the area. Almost all advertisements will invite you to send a stamped addressed envelope (s.a.e.) for details to the secretary, who in due course will send you back a schedule. Because of the cost, most organizers nowadays produce a duplicated schedule, which can be quite bulky, so be sensible and send an envelope that measures at least 23 × 10 cm (9 × 4 in).

Once the schedule arrives, make a note of the closing date for entries, and then work out which events you would like to have a go at. Be sure to get your entries to the secretary in time: late entries may not be accepted at all, and if they are accepted they usually cost extra.

Even beginners can usually find quite a variety of classes for which they are eligible. Gymkhana events are divided into age groups; jumping classes may include a minimus jumping, plus novice events for ponies of different heights. There will probably be clear round jumping, a handy pony class, and often one or other of the two jumping events which are regarded as gymkhana classes: Chase-me-Charlie and barrel elimination.

If you are eight years old or under and not absolutely confident that you can control your pony in a competition, you would probably be wise to enter the leading-rein gymkhana events, in which all competitors have to be led.

Most gymkhana events consist of the standard – and most popular – games. These include: bending, where you have to weave up and down a line of poles; potato or old sock races, where you have to collect potatoes or socks in turn and drop them in a bucket; flag races, in which you transfer coloured flags from one cone to another; and musical elimination games, such as musical mats or musical wands. Races which require little equipment are also popular with organizers – these include walking and trotting races, where you will be penalized if you go faster than the pace allowed, or run-and-lead, where you have to dismount from your pony half-way through the race and lead him to the finish.

Many of these games are included in the list for leading-rein competitors.

Chase-me-Charlie is a jumping event in which all competitors follow one another over one or two show jumps. The jumps start very low but are gradually raised as each competitor attempts them. Anyone who knocks down a jump or refuses is out. Eventually, the last survivors may be tackling jumps which are quite high, although, of course, any competitor may withdraw from the

Gymkhana games in action. **Above** Leaning low to ensure that the potato goes in the bucket. **Below** A bending race.

Above A mad dash to the centre in musical mats. **Below** A flag is whipped out of the cone during the flag race.

class if she thinks the jump has reached too great a height for herself or her pony to tackle.

In barrel elimination, competitors again follow one another over a jump, but this one consists of a row of oil drums. Gradually, the oil drums are removed until only one is left, and the winner is the pony which jumps it cleanly, without rapping it or side-stepping.

Some shows expect advance entries for jumping and showing classes but invite competitors to make entries for gymkhana events on the day. This means exactly what it says; you do not make any entries or send any entry fees for gymkhana events until you arrive at the show-ground. Clear round jumping is always entered on the day. This is not a competition in the sense that it produces winners, but it is a good way for someone who does not own any show jumps to try her pony out over a proper show-jumping course. You pay the entry fee to the steward in the collecting ring, ride round the course and collect a rosette if you finish the round without any penalties. You can have as many goes as you like as long as you pay the entry fee each time. The height of the course may be raised as the day progresses.

Handy pony competitions require entrants to complete a course of hazards, which may or may not include one or two jumps. You will probably have to transfer a sack or basket from one place to another, open and shut a gate, carry a bucket, hang out washing, lead your pony over a set of cavaletti, perhaps ride part of the course bareback; in fact, anything that the ingenuity of the organizers can devise. The course will be timed, penalties such as knocking down a jump will take the form of seconds added, and the winner is the one who completes the hazards in the fastest time. A handy pony competition is a good contest for sturdy, unflappable ponies which take everything in their stride but are not brilliant jumpers or very nippy gymkhana participants.

WHAT TO DO ON ARRIVAL

When you enter a show for the first time you may be worried about what you actually have to do as soon as you arrive on the show-ground.

The first point to remember is that you should arrive early. If it is a local show, within hacking distance, try to set off early enough to arrive at least half an hour before your first event. Your journey should be taken at an easy pace, so that your pony is not hot and tired before you get there and has plenty of energy for the forthcoming events. Take a headcollar with you, either strapped round your waist or on the pony under the bridle, and find a shady spot as soon as you arrive where you can tie up your pony. Unless your parents are following later in the car, you will have to take your picnic lunch and items from your grooming kit, such as a body brush and hoof-pick, in a satchel.

Collect your competitor's number from the secretary's tent or caravan. The number is printed on thin cardboard and has a piece of plastic string long enough to tie round your waist. Position it so that the number is displayed in the small of your back. You may be issued with a ticket for each event you enter and you have to give up the ticket to the steward when you go into the ring.

Check whether the show is running to time, especially if you have arrived after the show has started and your events are not due to begin until later in the day. It is not unusual for classes to start anything up to an hour or so late. If there is more than one arena or ring, find out which ring your events are in and where it is situated on the field. After that you can relax, find your friends and watch other competitors in action.

Your pony may well benefit from a period of warming up. Try to find a reasonably empty corner of the show-ground and put him quietly through his paces. There is usually a practice jump near the jumping arenas, but this is not an invitation to spend all day jumping. You should at all times think about your pony's welfare; never, for example, use him as a grandstand or gallop about the field to show everyone how fast he can go. The time for going fast is in the ring, not out of it.

Listen to loudspeaker announcements. Competitors for each event are usually called to the appropriate collecting ring about ten minutes before the event is due to begin. When you hear your class announced, make your way to the collecting point, but do not enter the arena until you are told to do so by the steward in charge.

Most gymkhana events are run in heats, with a final of six. Organizers have different methods of arranging the heats. Some leave it to the competitors, which means that all the good ones, who are well aware of the quality of the opposition, will try to avoid being in one heat together. Some heats are drawn, with competitors taking coloured counters out of a bag, so that all those with the same colour are put in the same heat.

Once you are in the ring for your heat, the judge or ring steward will briefly explain the rules. Do listen carefully at this stage; if you are disqualified later for contravening the rules, it is no use complaining that you didn't know or that this wasn't the rule that operated at the last show. Every judge is at liberty to alter the rules if she wishes and you must abide by the ones in force at that moment. If necessary, ask how many will be kept from each heat for the final; there is no point in tiring your pony unnecessarily by riding flat out to win if you are going to qualify anyway by coming second. Finalists are usually asked to wait in a corner until all the heats have finished. If you are lucky or skilled enough to make the final, jump off your pony, cross the stirrups over the saddle and rest your pony's back while you are waiting.

Finally, never complain at the judge's decision, even if you think you have been unfairly treated. The judges do their best to arbitrate fairly; maybe you did indeed beat the girl on the skewbald by a nose, but remember that next time there is a doubtful decision it might benefit you. At all shows you go to, it is possible to lodge an objection, but you will have to accompany it with a money deposit which will be forefeited if your objection is overruled. The only grounds on which you should object to another competitor is where you *know* the conditions of entry have been violated and can prove it – for example, if the rider is over age or the pony is over height.

Jumping classes, including minimus jumping (that is, for ponies of say 13.2 hh and under and riders aged 12 years and under), are normally run under standard rules. Each knock down counts four faults, the first refusal or run-out is three faults, the second six and the third, even if they are not all at the same jump, is elimination. If you take the wrong course or leave the arena before the round is finished (not unusual in novice classes where the pony can be wilful and the rider not firm enough) you will be eliminated.

Competitors with clear rounds, or equality of faults for first place, are invited to take part in a jump-off. This may be over the same course against the clock, over a raised course against the clock, or over a shortened and raised course against the clock. However it is organized, the jump-off is usually timed, and the pony with the lowest number of faults and the fastest round is the winner.

At the end of the day, hopefully with a number of rosettes and a pleasant sense of well-being, you have to ride home. Remember that your pony is tired, even though you may be feeling elated, and you should ride him home carefully and quietly. If necessary, get off and walk part of the way.

When you get home, remove the saddle and rub off the saddle marks, then turn him out into his field. He is better off being turned out straightaway than being put in a stable. Once in his familiar field, he can roll, have a drink and relax. Later on, after an hour or so, take him a feed.

The next day, catch him up and check him over for signs of stiffness. If you ride him, and there is no reason why you shouldn't, take him gently, just enough to work any stiffness out of him.

When you begin to go to shows and gymkhanas, you will no doubt stick to the local ones which are within easy hacking distance. However, in due course you will want to go to shows further afield and will need some form of transport to get there. By then, you will probably be ready for the next stage in your riding career, the acquisition of a second, competition, pony.

Pages 68–9 Vaulting on at speed may mean the difference between winning and losing. The sequence of actions starts with the first spring. Note the shortness of the rider's reins, so that her left hand is controlling the direction of the pony, while her right hand grasps the offside of the saddle flap helping the upward movement of her jump. The forward speed of the pony helps the rider to swing her right leg over the back of the saddle. By the end, she is already in the saddle, and her balance should be good enough for her not to need her feet in the stirrup-irons.

1

2

3

CHAPTER 8
The pony's health

Ponies are tough little creatures and, by and large, manage to remain remarkably healthy. As long as you follow the general rules of pony care, there is no reason why your pony should not lead a long and trouble-free life. And one of the first rules is to try to prevent illnesses before they arise.

INOCULATION

Horses can be given protection against tetanus and equine influenza with a single, annual injection.

Tetanus (also known as lockjaw) is an unpleasant, often fatal disease of the central nervous system, and it is very important that your pony is inoculated against it. It is caused by a germ which is found in the horse's intestines, in its dung, and often in the soil. In these places, it is harmless, but should it get into a suitable breeding site, such as a deep cut, it can breed and multiply. Puncture wounds, which are often hard to spot, are the most likely areas of infection. They provide the sort of airless conditions in which the tetanus germ flourishes. The incubation period for tetanus can be quite lengthy and an unprotected pony can develop tetanus long after the wound which caused the disease has cleared up.

The symptoms of tetanus are an inability to open the mouth (hence the alternative name, lockjaw), a tendency to shy at sudden sounds, head-jerking if the pony is flicked under the jaw, and the appearance in the eye of the third eyelid (or haw). Gradually, the pony finds it more and more difficult to move and his body becomes rigid, with forelegs and hind legs extended.

Luckily, inoculation is highly effective. After an initial dose and booster, the annual injection gives total immunity. As long as your pony's protection is kept up to date, there is no danger that the animal will become infected through a tiny, unnoticed cut.

Tetanus can also affect human beings, and it is one of the diseases which the ordinary routine injections guard against. Because you are going to spend much of your time around horses, however, it is sensible to visit your doctor and ask for a booster injection to be given to you.

The pony's anti-tetanus jab may be given alone or combined with an inoculation against equine influenza. The flu jab, in some people's eyes, is essential. Others believe that it does more harm than good. However, equine flu, while not fatal, is very infectious and can keep a pony off work for several weeks. The symptoms are fever and coughing, and the treatment is isolation, rest and a light diet.

If your pony is kept at livery, the stable-owner may insist on the inoculation, on the grounds that as the infection can spread quickly through the stables and prevent other horses from taking part in competitions it is better to provide whatever protection is available. Some places, such as racecourses and agricultural show-grounds, will not allow any horse to enter the premises without a valid vaccination certificate.

The initial two doses must be given between three weeks and three months apart, and these are followed by annual booster injections. After each injection the pony has to be rested for about a week, so you will have to plan the inoculation timetable to avoid any special events in which you could be hoping to take part. Most ponies show little reaction to the injection, although a few may seem lethargic for two or three weeks.

WORMING

Worming is another essential part of preventative medicine. All horses have parasites in their stomach and intestines. If they are there in very small quantities, the effect on the pony will be barely noticeable. Danger arises when the parasite count builds up.

Of the three types of worms found in horses, red worms (strongyles) are the most dangerous. A badly infested pony loses condition rapidly, looks thin and has a staring coat. He may suffer from anaemia and bouts of colic. Round worms are quite commonly found in horses, and tapeworms are occasionally present.

The parasites form a continuous cycle. Worm eggs are passed out of the pony in his droppings. As the pony grazes, he picks up the larvae and swallows them. They hatch out in his stomach and live on the food which should be nourishing the pony.

A field which is continuously grazed by horses can become severely infected with parasites, and these can affect all the ponies which live in it. The first line of attack is to care for the field properly. This means using any of the remedies which will break the worm cycle: picking up droppings regularly, cutting and harrowing, resting the field, or grazing sheep or cattle in it for a time.

The second is to worm the pony. Worm powders and pastes can be bought from the vet, who will advise you on the best sort to buy and the amount you will need for the size of your pony.

Powders are easily administered as they are tasteless and can be mixed with the pony's feed. Pastes come in throwaway syringes. The syringe is inserted into the corner of the pony's mouth and the paste squirted on to his tongue. Most ponies should be wormed every eight to ten weeks.

Bot-flies can also be treated with a worming paste or powder. The bot-fly lays its eggs on the pony's coat, usually down the legs and on the shoulders and flanks. They are noticeable in late summer, especially on a dark-coloured pony, showing up as dozens of little yellow specks. No amount of brushing will remove them, although they can be painstakingly picked off with the finger-nails or a safety razor.

As the eggs start hatching, they seem to cause irritation, making the pony lick or nibble at his legs. As he does this, he swallows the grubs and they attach themselves to the stomach wall. They stay there for several months, interfering with the pony's digestion, until eventually, the following spring, they pass out of the pony in his droppings.

Anti-bot-fly granules or paste can be given to the pony in the late autumn. These kill the grubs while they are in the stomach. It may be difficult, however, to get your pony to accept the granules, even when they are mixed thoroughly with his feed, and the paste and syringe method of application may be the only effective one to use.

PROBLEMS WHICH CAN AFFECT A PONY AT GRASS

Spring is the time to be especially vigilant in the care of your pony, as there are various problems which can crop up.

Lice

Lice increase rapidly as the weather gets warmer. These little, wingless insects collect in the hair roots of the mane and tail and cause intense irritation as they hatch. The pony rubs the affected parts against fence posts and tree trunks in an effort to relieve the itching and often rubs away portions of the mane and tail as well.

If you suspect an outbreak of lice, inspect the mane and tail area thoroughly and take advice if you are not absolutely sure what you are looking for. Lice can sometimes be mistaken for scurf. Treatment is by means of louse powder, or the use of a wash or spray. The powder should be worked well into the hair with the fingers. Only the hatched lice will be killed, however, and you should repeat the treatment ten days or a fortnight later to catch any new hatchings.

Laminitis

This is another common problem with grass-fed ponies. Its basic cause is overfeeding and under-exercise, and is most likely to occur in the spring when a pony gorges himself to bursting on the new grass. Laminitis is sometimes called fever of the foot or founder. It gets its name from the laminae, layers of

71

Above Care of the feet is an important part of pony care. The hooves should be picked out every day. For a show, they can be oiled to smarten them up.
Opposite Ponies are tough, and manage to remain remarkably healthy. If you follow the general rules of pony care, there is no reason why your pony should not lead a long and trouble-free life.

tissue which separate the pedal bone from the wall of the hoof. These become greatly inflamed and the effect on the pony is like having to force a badly swollen foot into a very tight shoe. Not surprisingly, a pony with laminitis is extremely reluctant to move.

The first sign of laminitis is when the pony, while standing in the field, pushes his forelegs far forward so that his weight is taken on the heels. He may rest the front feet in turn. Laminitis always starts in the front feet but it can spread to the back ones as well. A pony with the disease in all four feet will throw all his weight back on to the heels. The outer wall of each affected hoof will feel hot.

It is essential to get the pony back to a stable, but this is easier said than done and will certainly take a long time. Some relief

from the pain can be gained by cooling the feet with water, either by trickling water from a hose on to the hooves, or by standing the pony in a stream of running water. As a last resort, you could try placing each foot in turn in a bowl of cold water.

You should call the vet as soon as you have managed to get the pony into a stable. Modern drugs can help the condition by reducing the inflammation and easing the pain. Other remedies include removing the pony's shoes and encouraging him to walk about in order to improve the circulation. A vital ingredient in the recovery process is putting the pony on a very restricted diet.

It may be several weeks before the pony gets better and can move freely again without pain. Even then, the feet may be left with dropped soles and ridges of horn round the hoof. The blacksmith's help will be needed in getting the feet into good shape again.

When a pony has had laminitis once, he can easily get it again, and care must be taken to see that he never gets too fat nor has access to too much rich grass. In spring, this may mean bringing the pony into a stable and keeping him without food for hours at a time. Alternatively, he may be turned out into a paddock which is almost bare of grass.

Always remember, too, that laminitis can occur at any time of the year. Too much food of any sort, coupled with insufficient work to burn up the calories, can put the pony at risk.

Sweet itch

Sweet itch is a condition that occurs only during the summer. If you bought your pony during the winter months, you may not have realized that he is prone to it. Unfortunately, it is a chronic complaint and, although various forms of treatment exist and will no doubt be suggested by friends, there is no absolutely foolproof remedy.

Sweet itch is a skin complaint, believed to be caused by an allergic reaction to a particular type of biting insect. The effect is an acute irritation of the mane and tail area and around the face, causing the pony to rub himself against the nearest available tree or post until he produces sores. In the early evenings, when the insects are at their worst, he will trot round and round the field in a futile attempt to get away from the midges' attentions.

The most successful remedy is to stable the

pony by day and turn him into his field after dark, but unless stable and field are close at hand, this is not always possible. Benzyl benzoate or sulphanilamide may be applied to the sores and various fly-repellents may give temporary protection. In very severe cases, the vet may suggest cortisone injections to try and overcome the allergy. Sweet itch starts around May or June and continues until the autumn.

Galls

Galls or sores sometimes occur with soft, grass-fed ponies and are caused by chafing, either by the saddle or by the girth. Salt-and-water solution (one dessert-spoon of salt to 57 cl (UK 1 pt; USA 2½ cups) of water) can help to dry up the sores, but you should also look for the cause. If necessary, have the saddle re-stuffed or change the girth and wait until the galls are healed before using the saddle again. The salt-and-water solution will help to harden the skin.

Coughing

This is not necessarily a sign of illness but it always requires investigation. If a pony coughs once or twice at the start of a ride or when the weather is dry and dusty, he may simply be clearing a tickle from his throat. If the cough persists, especially if the pony has a runny nose, suspect some sort of infection and call the vet. Do not ride the pony.

Too much exertion when the pony has a cough can lead to the chronic condition known as broken wind. This means that some of the lung cavities have broken down; a cure is not possible although you can prevent the condition from getting worse. Essentially it means that he is only capable of light work; he must never be ridden hard, he must not be allowed to eat, even grass, for an hour before a ride, and his hay should be dampened before it is given to him. He needs plenty of fresh air and will do better living out than in a stable.

Broken wind is caused by riding a coughing pony before the cough has cleared up or by galloping unfit, grass-fed ponies.

A persistent cough with no other symptoms may be caused by lung worms. A laboratory test on the pony's dung will indicate the presence of lung worms and the vet will prescribe powders or paste to get rid of them. Ponies rarely pick up lung worms and if they

do so it is almost certainly because they have come into contact with donkeys, which are common carriers of the parasite even when they themselves are unaffected.

Sweating

A grass-fed pony will sweat easily, especially if he has a thick winter coat. When you return from a ride, always give the pony time to cool down by walking the last half-mile (1km) home before you turn him out into the field. If you have to stand around in a chill wind with a sweating pony, walk him about quietly and cover his loins with a rug or coat.

The first thing a pony does when he is loose in his field is to get down on the ground and roll. This is perfectly normal and nothing to worry about even if he rolls more than once.

When a pony sweats for no obvious reason, he may be ill and you should look for other symptoms. Listlessness, trembling, dull eyes, loss of appetite are all signs that something is wrong, and you should call the vet. If a sweating pony keeps kicking or biting at his stomach, is restless and keeps getting down, rolling and getting up again, he is displaying all the signs of _colic_, which is indigestion. Colic can be caused by a number of things: overeating, eating poor quality food, drinking too much and too soon after a meal, exercising too soon after eating, or it may have a more serious cause.

Whatever the reason, professional help is essential. While you are waiting for the vet to arrive, try to keep the pony warm by covering him with rugs and, if necessary, holding a hot-water bottle to his belly. You should try to get him into a stable (if you have none of your own, most horse-owners will be willing to help a pony in distress) where he will have to stay until he recovers. If you can, keep him moving and try not to let him roll. He rolls to relieve the pain, but if he throws himself about too severely, he could twist a gut.

Fortunately, colic does not happen very often, particularly if you are vigilant in your care of the pony.

LAMENESS

Ponies can go lame for a variety of reasons, from a simple bruising of the sole to a severe sprain. Lameness is not easy to detect, especially if it is slight, but it will show up best at a trot. The pony should be trotted along a hard, level surface and watched from in front and behind. If the injury is in a foreleg, the pony will raise his head when the unsound leg hits the ground and nod downwards on the sound one. In a hind leg, the quarters on the sound side will droop more than the lame side.

Unless the cause of the lameness is obvious, such as a cut or swelling, look first at the hoof. Pick out the feet to satisfy yourself that the pony has not picked up a stone or nail, and tap the sole gently to check that there is no inflammation. A call to the vet is always a good precaution.

TEETHING PROBLEMS

The most common cause of eating difficulties lies with the teeth. A horse's teeth are constantly growing, but the rate of growth is usually matched by the rate of wear. Sometimes, however, and this is particularly prevalent in older ponies, the teeth do not wear down quickly enough and grow too long. You should always suspect this if your pony takes a long time over his food or drops bits out while he is eating, a practice known as quidding. Ask the vet to inspect the teeth and, if necessary, to rasp them down.

Part II
Competition Pony

CHAPTER 9
Choosing a second pony

Sooner or later, the time will come when you have grown out of your first pony. The reason may be purely physical – a long-legged thirteen-year-old looks silly on a 12 hh pony – but, far more likely, you are now capable of doing much more than your pony is.

You will, for example, be entering a variety of competitions, from gymkhana classes to cross-country events. You will reach an age when the fences in the jumping events open to you are too high for your little pony, and although he is quite able to carry your weight out hacking he does not have the scope for anything more ambitious.

The moment of decision comes around the age of twelve or thirteen. At twelve, you are still eligible for most minimus jumping classes or for the 12.2 hh and under junior jumping and showing events. Once you reach thirteen, however, the only showing class left open to you if you have a small pony is the working hunter pony under 13 hh.

Most children try to put off the decision as long as possible, especially if their first pony has given them faithful service for many years. Some children are able to pass the pony on to a younger brother or sister; a few decide to keep him just for gymkhana and handy pony events. But for those who cannot afford to keep more than one pony at a time, a new home must be found for the first pony and a search started for the second.

FINDING A SECOND PONY

Second ponies are found in exactly the same way as first ones: through word of mouth, advertisements in horse magazines, dealers, or at auctions. But you do have an advantage over those far-off days when you first acquired a pony of your own. You probably know people through the Pony Club and local shows, and it will be much easier to spread the word around that you are looking for a pony. You probably also have a better idea of the sort of pony you are looking for.

Someone older than you may be in much the same position as you are, ready to sell their pony and move on to something bigger, but reluctant to do so because they are anxious to find a good home. The knowledge that you are in the market could just be the factor that encourages them to approach you. Similarly, someone else might come to you and ask if you would sell your present pony. A great many transactions take place without the ponies concerned ever being advertised at all.

It is, of course, important to decide exactly what type of pony you want. If you still enjoy gymkhana games but are beginning to get a taste for show-jumping or cross-country courses, then you must find an all-round pony – one which is nimble enough to nip in and out of bending poles, but bold enough to tackle a drop fence, a big spread or to go through water with confidence. Perhaps you like the discipline of dressage and would prefer a suitable one-day eventer or a combined training specialist. Or perhaps you fancy the idea of all these competitions but have been frustrated so far by the limitations of your present pony.

People have mixed feelings about buying a known pony from their own area. On the one hand, you have the advantage of knowing what a pony can do, and forewarning of all its habits. On the other hand, there is the possibility that you might not get on as well with the pony as its current owner does. There is nothing more shattering to one's self-confidence than to overhear someone saying, 'Of course, that pony did terribly well when Angela had him; can't think what's happened to him now,' just when you have completed a dreadful show-jumping round and are beginning to wonder the same thing yourself.

If you buy a pony from another part of the country, the chances are that no one locally knows his reputation. If you do well, you can take much of the credit yourself; if you do badly, you have not lost face.

Unless you have contacts, such as friends or relations, in a distant part of the country, the best place to find a new pony is through magazine advertisements. An advertisement will give the pony's height and age. It will also state the activities that the pony has taken part in or been successful at.

Standard abbreviations are used in advertisements to describe these activities, and you should be familiar with them. They are listed in Appendix III page 191. Remember that the greater the pony's achievements, the higher his price is likely to be.

In addition to describing the pony's achievements the advertisement will emphasize a pony's good points; for example, quiet to box, shoe, clip, and so on. Sometimes, the phrase 'Not a novice ride' is included and this, of course, is open to various interpretations. It could mean that the pony is lively and needs firm handling but is generally viceless; or that it is liable to belt off at the least provocation, has a mouth like leather and needs someone with enormous strength to keep it even half-way under control. You cannot tell which category applies until you try out the pony and, even then, you should ask the sellers to explain exactly what they mean. Never forget that while people may put only half-truths in an advertisement, it is difficult for them to tell a downright lie if asked a direct question.

What you are no doubt looking for in your second pony is a bigger, faster and more capable replica of the one that you have already. Forget it! Every pony is different, and each time you buy one you are buying a unique individual, with his own temperament and characteristics. You will have to get to know him just as you got to know your first pony.

Many riders expect to get on a new pony and have him perform as well as he did with his previous owner. However, a relationship between pony and rider does not develop overnight; it may be six months or more before the two of you are going well together.

Sometimes, it is true, the transition from one owner to the next is smooth and trouble-free. On the other hand, you may find that it goes well to begin with and then, for no obvious reason, things go wrong. The pony develops a tendency to stop or run out at a jump; instead of being lively and on the bit, he falls behind; he may take charge when you are out on a ride, or suddenly decide that he can't go without company.

There may be a number of reasons for the change. Perhaps you have altered his diet — try increasing his intake of energy-producing food; perhaps he has developed a liking for another pony in the field and gets upset if he has to go anywhere without him. Most probably, the reason is that you do not ride the pony exactly as his previous owner did. If your last pony had only to be pointed at a jump in order to jump it, you probably think that is how all ponies should be ridden round a jumping course. You have forgotten that some ponies need to be told exactly how to tackle a fence, the speed they should go at, and the moment of take-off. If your last pony rushed his fences and had to be held back until the final moment it is no good using the same method with a pony that loses impulsion if he is checked at the wrong time.

Some ponies are naturally confident. Others take their cue from their rider. If you think as you approach a jump, 'That looks big; we'll never get over it,' your pony may sense your feelings and believe that you know best. Result: a refusal. Why should he jump something that even his rider is frightened of?

At this stage, it is more important than ever that you should continue to take regular riding lessons. An experienced instructor will be able to tell you where you are going wrong and help you to put things right.

SELLING YOUR OLD PONY

Whether you sell your pony locally to friends or acquaintances, or to strangers who live far away, depends on how much you mind seeing your pony in someone else's care.

The advantage of a local sale is that you will

already know something about the pony's new home and can feel confident that he will be properly looked after. If you sell him to strangers, you must face up to the fact that he is going out of your life, probably for ever.

Many people worry that if they advertise the pony he may end up on the meat market. Obviously, there is no guarantee that the man who buys your pony and tells you that it is a present for his daughter is not a slaughter-man, but you can take some steps to check where your pony is going.

For example, once the sale has been agreed, insist that the pony is not collected until, say, the following week, or if your family has a trailer, offer to deliver the pony yourselves. In the meantime, visit the new home, if it is within reasonable distance, and check on the conditions he will be living in. If you have friends in the area, ask if they know of the family concerned. People quickly acquire a reputation – whether good or bad – in the horse world.

You are perfectly entitled to ask the would-be purchasers if they have ever owned a pony before, but there is no need to be put off by those who admit inexperience. After all, you were in that situation yourself once. Ask whether the new owner is a member of the Pony Club, and urge them to join if they have not already done so. You can also ask to visit the pony from time to time. No genuine buyer would object to that.

It is up to you whether you sell your pony with all his tack or not. If you are getting a bigger pony, there is probably no reason to keep the first pony's saddle and bridle, and at least you would know that he will be wearing tack that fits him.

Some people always have the pony shod before the sale and bring his inoculations and worming up to date. That way, they can be sure that they have done the very best for the pony.

The day he leaves is bound to be a sad one, especially if you have had him for a long time. But once you have grown out of a pony, it is not a good idea to keep him purely for senti-mental reasons. Ponies are happiest when they are working, in a home where they are loved and cared for. Your pony's new owners should be able to give him all the attention which you, with your next pony, might not have time for.

LENDING A PONY

It has become a common practice nowadays to let a pony go out on loan rather than to sell him. Provided you do not need the cash which selling him would produce, it is quite a good method by which your pony can lead a useful life without your having to say goodbye to him altogether.

Before lending the pony, make certain that you and his new 'owner' have agreed on all the details of the arrangement. Decide before-hand who is to be responsible for the feed bills, vet's bills, farrier's fees, and so on. Decide on the period of the loan. Sometimes it is better to fix a limit of, say, two years than to let the pony go for an indefinite time.

Make a list of everything that you are sending with him: saddle, including girths and stirrup-irons and leathers, bridle, head-collar, lead-rope, and so on. Settle which of you is to make the ultimate decision should the pony have an accident or become so ill that he has to be humanely destroyed. Do bear in mind that such a decision sometimes has to be made very quickly. A pony should not have to suffer longer than necessary because you are away on holiday and cannot be contacted.

When you have agreed the terms, write them down. Prepare two copies of the agree-ment and get the signatures of both parties on each copy.

Then let your pony go with a light heart. You have a new pony now to focus your love and attention on.

When the time comes to get a new pony, you must think carefully about what kind of pony you want. If you are developing a taste for show-jumping and cross-country courses, you will need a pony who can tackle fences confidently.

CHAPTER 10
Stabling

When you progress to a second pony, and especially if you intend to enter competitions, the question arises as to the best method of keeping him. Your previous pony lived out all the year round. When you went to gymkhanas, you caught him early in the morning, groomed him as best you could, spent the day at the show and turned him out in his field again in the evening.

The system worked very well and your pony remained healthy. His thick winter coat protected him during the winter months, and the field shelter gave him relief from the flies and hot sun in summer. Of course, he did tend to sweat up a little in the winter, especially when you took him to the Pony Club meet, and it was often annoying on gymkhana days to find a wet pony in the field when it had rained the night before. But at the level of competitions you were tackling, none of this really mattered. In any case, it was the same for everyone.

Now you have a new pony, and you are becoming more ambitious. When you go to a show, you want your pony to look immaculate. The last thing you want is a grey coat disfigured by grass stains or a tail clogged with burrs. A stable can prevent this. Your pony will still spend most of his time out-of-doors, but you can bring him in for the night before a show. In winter, you can have him partially clipped and keep him in at night and out by day. You can regulate his intake of food much more closely.

This is the time to consider building a stable or converting an outbuilding into a loose box. If your parents are willing to buy a ready-made stable, collect as much information as you can so that you can tell them exactly what you need. There are a number of manufacturers of sectional stables, and most of them advertise in the horse magazines. They will send you pamphlets and price lists on request, and by comparing the various designs, you will be able to form an idea of your own requirements.

The most basic form of stable available is a simple loose box fitted with a pitched roof, window and divided door. In some designs, the front of the roof is extended to form an overhang which helps to shelter the stable from rain and sun. It is essential that the stable has good guttering, but kicking boards lining the inside walls are necesarry only if your pony is going to spend much of his time in the stable.

Prices include delivery and erection but not the preparation of the site. You will have to make separate arrangements to lay down a concrete base. Whether planning permission is needed or not depends on your local authority, but a visit to the local planning office will provide all the necessary information.

If you are hoping, in due course, to buy a horse, it is sensible to get a loose box big enough for a hunter. The ideal size is 4.3 × 3.6 m (14 × 12 ft), which gives a big horse plenty of room to move around in. For a pony, 3.6 × 3 m (12 × 10 ft) would be ample. Much, however, depends on what you can afford.

The stable should not open towards the prevailing wind. South or south-east would probably be best, especially if the roof has an overhang.

The conversion of an existing outbuilding is

a cheaper alternative to starting from scratch. Many older houses have a brick-built garage or shed which is not being used for a car, and as the following example shows these can be converted into a stable without too much trouble. The existing building had three brick walls beneath a pitched roof and a large, sliding, wooden door across the front. The door provided enough material to make a fourth wall over one half of the open side and a properly hung, divided stable door to fit the other half. The existing concrete floor was in good condition and already had a small groove, which would provide drainage. Some parts of the brick walls were repointed. The stable was finished off with a coat of dark brown paint on the lower half of the inside walls and a coat of white paint on the upper half. Although the stable has no window, the white paint inside makes it light and airy; the darker paint below makes it easier to keep clean.

STABLE FITTINGS

A loose box needs very few fittings. The most important, of course, are rings to which you can tie either haynets or the pony. These need to be bolted right through the wall to be completely secure. A manger is useful, but it should be removable so that it can be cleaned out from time to time. Bucket holders can be bought, but an old car tyre is just as effective for preventing a bucket of water or feed from being knocked over.

Doors should be secured with bolts. The bottom door needs two bolts, of which the lower one should be a kick bolt that can be operated with the foot. One bolt is sufficient for the top door. Both doors need hooks and staples to hold them back when they are wide open. The doorway should be at least 1.25 m (4 ft) wide so that a horse or pony can pass through without banging himself. The doors should open outwards.

If your stable is fitted with electric lighting – and it is extremely useful to have safe, artficial lighting available – ensure that the bulb is well out of reach of the pony. A bulkhead light is best for a wall-fitting. For safety's sake, the switch should be outside the stable; a properly insulated, exterior light-switch is best.

If you use a hay-rack rather than a haynet, do not fix it to the wall above the height of the pony's head. The old-fashioned system of high-level hay-racks is now regarded as un-

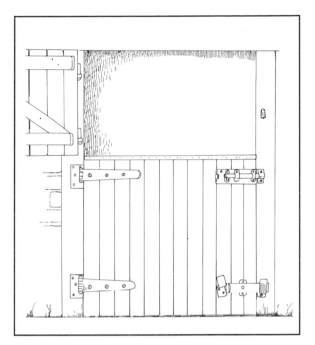

A stable door should be divided, so that the top half can be left open to provide ventilation. The bottom half needs bolts top and bottom to be really secure as many ponies learn to undo any bolts they can reach.

comfortable for the horse and even dangerous, because of the risk of hay seeds and dust falling into his eyes.

BEDDING

When a pony is to spend a night in a stable he will need some form of bedding. Wood-shavings and straw are the two most popular forms, but peat moss is a good alternative.

Wood-shavings These are usually sold compressed into plastic-covered bales. They are easy to stack and, provided the plastic has not split, can be stored out-of-doors. Some firms sell the shavings more loosely packed in hessian sacks, but these need to be covered over if they are kept in the open air. Compressed shavings need separating out with a fork or by hand so that they do not form a lumpy bed; the loose shavings only need raking over.

Shavings are sometimes combined with sawdust for economy, in which case the sawdust is put down first. Always cover any drains in the stable before putting down sawdust, so that they do not get clogged up. When raking over sawdust and shavings, check that they do not contain old nails or sharp off-cuts of wood which might harm your pony.

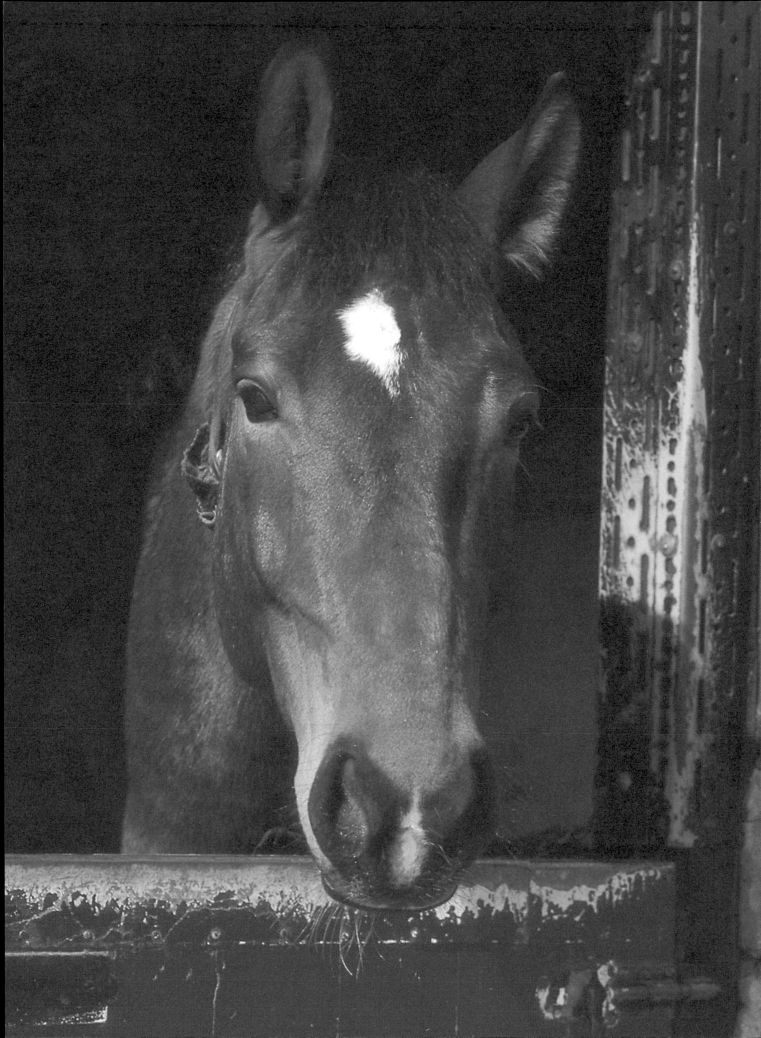

Straw The best type of straw for bedding is *wheat straw*, because it is warm and comfortable and drains well. It is usually quite easy and cheap to obtain. *Oat straw* is more porous and therefore gets wet and soggy quite quickly. Ponies do tend to eat it, however, just as they will *barley straw*, although the latter makes good bedding provided it has been made by a combine harvester and is free of prickly awns.

Peat moss This tends to be dusty when it is first laid but it is less of a fire hazard than straw or shavings. It needs to be raked regularly to prevent it from becoming hard-packed.

Bedding is necessary in a stable not only to give the pony a soft surface to lie down on, but also to provide insulation and to prevent the pony's legs from being jarred through standing on a hard floor.

Care of bedding

When a pony has spent a few hours in a stable, some of his bedding will have become wet and soiled. This must be replaced by fresh material.

With a straw bed, the old clean straw should be separated from the rest and piled in a corner. After the dirty straw has been taken away, sweep the floor and allow it to air before re-laying the bed and adding new straw.

With shavings and moss, the droppings and wet patches are forked into a wheelbarrow or skip and the bedding raked to keep it sweet.

Laying a bed

It is a false economy to stint on the amount of bedding used. As a pony moves round his stable, the bedding will be shifted about. If it was very sparse to start with, this will produce bare patches of floor, with the risk to the pony of capped hocks or elbows from lying on concrete. So make the bed as thickly as you can. Shake up the straw to make it springy and comfortable and pile a double layer around the edges as a precaution against injury and draughts. Shavings and peat moss should also be piled higher against the walls.

If your time is limited, you can use the *deep litter* system. Only the droppings are re-

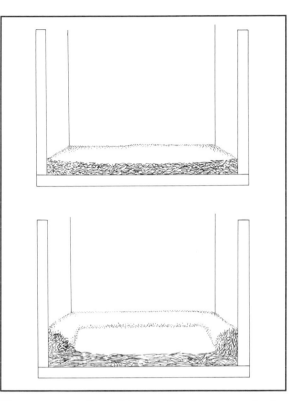

The wrong and the right way of laying a straw bed. **Top:** incorrect. **Bottom:** correct. The straw has been banked around the edges to protect the pony from draughts and risk of injury.

moved each time and fresh material is added to the existing bed. In time, the bed will become very deep and eventually, say every three to four months, you will have to take out the whole lot and begin again. However, removing the entire bed from a stable which has been in regular use for about fifteen weeks is a heavy task.

If you will not be using the stable very often, you should re-do the bed on each occasion. While the stable is empty, heap the existing, unsoiled bedding into one corner and leave the floor clean and aired.

KEEPING A PONY IN AT NIGHT

If you plan to work your pony quite hard during the winter, hunting regularly or taking him to indoor shows, it is sensible to have him partially clipped, so that he will not sweat up too much when he is working, and to keep him in by night and out by day. The dark evenings will prevent you from exercising him during the week, but he will get

If a pony is in a stable all day, it is important that he can look out and watch whatever is going on in the yard.

enough exercise for himself if he is in a field by day. You can ensure that he is warm and well fed at night by bringing him into the stable when you get home from school. Remember to keep the top half of the stable door open at all times.

There is usually no need to start this routine until winter arrives, but once you have started it you will have to carry on until the following April. If there are likely to be any problems – if your pony's field, for example, is a long way from his loose box – it is better to keep him turned out permanently and provide him with a field shelter, rather than to use a stable.

Depending on the clip you choose (see page 131), it may be necessary to put the pony in a New Zealand rug whenever he is turned out in a field. An unclipped pony or one with a belly clip only, will not require either a New Zealand rug or a night rug.

The combined system – field by day, stable by night – takes up more time than if you visit your pony in his field to feed him. The stable has to be mucked out and the new bed laid, and if this has to be done in daylight hours, you may find that your winter timetable gets very rushed. Whether you get the stable ready in the morning or wait until after school depends on how good you are at getting up early. On the whole, it is probably easier to muck out in the morning, and the before-school routine need not take more than fifteen or twenty minutes.

Firstly, take some hay out to the pony's field (for quantity, see page 87): you can give it either in a haynet or spread on the ground. Then return to the stable, remove the pony's night rug (if he wears one) and pick out his feet. Put his New Zealand rug on him, and turn him into the field. Return to the stable again, remove all the soiled straw or shavings to the muck-heap and prepare the new bed. Fill the night's haynets and hang up. Empty and rinse out the water buckets and refill. Hang the night rug in a dry, airy place, say goodbye to your pony, and get back to breakfast and school.

The longest job is the mucking out of the stable. If you can manage to complete this in the morning, all you have to do in the evening is to prepare the pony's short feed, swap his rugs over and put him into his box for the night. That takes up very little time and you should have no difficulty in fitting it into after-school activities, such as extra work, music lessons or club meetings.

DISPOSAL OF MANURE

Well-rotted stable manure is a blessing to gardeners. If you keep a well-ordered muck-heap, you will be able to sell bags of compost, which provides a handy source of pocket-money. If possible, build your heap on a concrete base and preferably make two bays so that one can be left to rot while you are filling the other. A proprietary compost maker can be added to encourage decomposition. Straw rots down more quickly than wood-shavings.

CHAPTER 11
Feeding

Hay should always form the major portion of a pony's winter diet, whatever work he is doing. It may also be necessary to feed hay in a very hot summer when the available grass has dried up and turned brown.

Hay alone, however, will not provide sufficient energy for a pony taking part regularly in shows, gymkhanas, hunting, or Pony Club activities. The feeding programme should then include some combination of concentrates.

Most diet sheets for ponies and horses are worked out in relation to the animal's body weight, and weight is also used to measure the quantity of food to be given. The winter feed table below gives a rough guide to a pony's needs, but it is open to a number of variations as no two ponies' requirements are exactly the same.

Getting the diet right for your own pony will depend on trial and error. If, for example, your pony appears to be losing weight, although he is healthy in all other respects and his worming programme is up to date, his intake of concentrates will have to be stepped up. If he is lively, choose a food such as barley that puts on flesh without making him excitable. If he seems to 'run out of puff' quite quickly, give him some extra oats.

Introduce changes in his diet gradually and be guided as far as possible by the pony himself. If his haynet is emptied between one feeding time and the next, he may be getting too little. As far as hay is concerned it is always better to offer too much. A spring balance hanging in your feed room will give you an accurate reading of the amount of hay you are offering.

When measuring dry feeds, use scales to weigh the quantity contained in, say, one

Winter feed table for a pony wholly at grass or stabled by night		
Pony's height	Hay	Concentrates
Under 11 hh	2.2–3.6 kg (5–8 lb)	Cubes 450 g (1 lb) Bran 225 g (∂ lb) Sugar-beet 225 g (∂ lb)
11–12.2 hh	3.6–4.5 kg (8–10 lb)	Cubes 900 g (2 lb) Bran 450 g (1 lb) Sugar-beet 450 g (1 lb)
12.3–13.2 hh	4.5–5.4 kg (10–12 lb)	Cubes 1.4 kg (3 lb) Bran 450 g (1 lb) Sugar-beet 700 g (1∂ lb)
13.3–14.2 hh	5.4–6.4 kg (12–14 lb)	Cubes 1.8 kg (4 lb) Bran 450 g (1 lb) Sugar-beet 900 g (2 lb)

heaped scoopful. Provided you always use the same scoop, there is no need to weigh accurately each time, but do not be tempted to give a little more for luck.

Sugar-beet, either as pulp or as cubes, should be weighed dry, but it must be soaked for twelve to twenty-four hours before being fed. Oats may be substituted for cubes but the quantity of oats should be less. Allow 450 g (1 lb) of oats for 700 g (1½ lb) of cubes. Other forms of concentrate may be substituted according to your pony's tastes, but try not to exceed the total quantity by weight for each feed. Root crops and apples are always popular with ponies and can be added to the feed at any time.

CONCENTRATES

Cubes
There are various types of cubes on the market. They contain a mixture of many ingredients, including vitamins. The manufacturer's leaflet will tell you what the cubes contain and you should follow the maker's recommendation for your particular pony. Some cubes, for example, contain more protein than others and a high protein cube could be dangerous for your pony. Most ponies like cubes, but you should always mix them with dampened bran or chaff before giving them to your pony. This will ensure that he eats slowly, digesting them properly. Never buy too much at one time as cubes will deteriorate in store. Storage time: approximately three months. Cubes are a good feed for ponies as they are less heating than oats.

Oats
This is the traditional food for horses. Good oats have large, hard, clean grains. They may be fed whole but are more easily digested if they are bruised, rolled or crushed. However, crushed oats can go stale quite quickly and should be used within three to four weeks. Chaff or bran should be mixed with the oats before feeding. Oats can make ponies quite excitable and should therefore be fed to ponies with care.

Barley
This is a very good winter food for ponies kept at grass, as it keeps them fat and well without getting them hotted up. Whole barley grains have a very hard and indigestible covering which must be broken down before being fed to horses. If you buy rolled, crushed or flaked barley, or pre-cooked (micronized) barley, this will already have been done.

If you buy whole-grain barley, it must be simmered in water for four to six hours to soften the grains before you feed it to your pony. If whole grains pass out in the droppings, the barley is not being cooked for long enough. This is an inconvenient way of feeding barley. It is tedious, and it creates an unpleasant smell while it is cooking. However, it is an excellent feed for fattening thin horses, and for tempting poor eaters.

Flaked maize
This should always be used sparingly as, although it is good for fattening purposes, it can overheat the pony's blood. It is often an ingredient in proprietary mixtures and other combined feeds. Although in the UK maize is always fed flaked, in the USA it is fed whole or on the cob.

Beans
Dried beans are nutritious, but are considered too heating for ponies. A small handful mixed with the pony's other feed may be beneficial in winter if the pony lives out. Beans are usually bruised or split before feeding. If in doubt, it is best to leave beans out of your pony's diet.

Sugar-beet
Dried sugar-beet is sold as pulp or as cubes and it provides both energy and roughage. It is an excellent winter feed for ponies that are kept mainly at grass, and is always very popular with them. *It is essential to soak dried sugar-beet before use.* Place the pulp or cubes in a bucket and add water at the rate of approximately 2½ parts water to 1 part pulp, or 4 parts water to 1 part cubes. Soak for twelve to twenty-four hours. Never soak more sugar-beet than will be fed. Sugar-beet starts to ferment as soon as it is mixed with water and the fermentation must not be allowed to continue for too long. After soaking, always pour away any surplus liquid before mixing with chaff, bran and other feeds.

Dry sugar-beet should never be fed to a pony. It swells considerably on contact with water or other liquids, and it would be dangerous if this happened in the pony's stomach. Take care to keep dried sugar-beet cubes away from other cubes to avoid muddling them up.

Bran

This is made from wheat-husk. The most suitable type for ponies is known as broad bran. It should smell fresh and be free of lumps. Its main purpose is to give bulk to the feed and to encourage the pony to eat slowly. It should be dampened before being fed. Wet bran has a laxative effect on horses, dry bran the reverse.

Bran mash

This is a good pick-me-up for a tired pony or one that is off-colour. It is made by filling a bucket about three-quarters full of bran and adding boiling water until the bran is thoroughly wet. The bucket should then be covered with a thick cloth or hessian sack and left to 'cook' slowly while it cools. Once it is cool enough for the pony to eat, stir in about 55 g (2 oz) of salt, a few oats or some crushed barley, and a spoonful of molasses or black treacle, diluted in warm water.

Oatmeal gruel

This is another useful tonic for a tired pony after a hard day's work, provided the pony will take it. Simply put a double handful of oatmeal into a bucket, and add enough boiling water to make a thin gruel. Stir well. Leave it to cool. It should be thin enough for the pony to drink.

Linseed

As a general conditioner and means of making the coat shine, linseed would be hard to beat. Its drawback is that it takes a while to prepare. It has to be cooked properly as raw linseed is poisonous to horses. If you wish to improve your pony's coat during the winter, linseed can be made into a jelly and added to the feed once a week. To make the jelly, put 110–225 g (4–8 oz) of linseed in a saucepan, cover it with water and leave the pan in a warm place, such as a very cool oven, until the next day. Then add more water and bring to the boil. Allow it to boil for ten to fifteen minutes before taking the saucepan from the heat and leaving it to cool. As it cools, the linseed sets into a *jelly*, which you mix with your pony's feed. It is very important that the water containing the linseed should boil. If you add extra water at the second stage, but still bring it to the boil, the result will be linseed *tea*, which can be mixed with bran to make a linseed mash.

Chaff

This is simply hay, sometimes mixed with a small quantity of oat straw, which has been passed through a giant mincing machine and chopped into small pieces. It is sometimes called chop for that reason. The mincing machine or 'chaff cutter' is a useful piece of equipment for stables with several horses, but it is not worth the expense if you have only one or two ponies to look after. Instead, ready-prepared chaff can usually be bought from a corn merchant. The purpose of chaff is to add bulk to a short feed, encouraging the pony to eat more slowly. Some greedy ponies gobble their food so quickly that some of the nutritional value is lost.

Mixtures

There are various ready-mixed foods on the market and they are quite useful for ponies which do not like cubes. They look like breakfast food and contain oats, cubes, flaked maize and bran in balanced proportions, as well as added vitamins and minerals. Some also contain molasses to make them more palatable for finicky feeders. If you choose a well-known brand, you can be sure that your pony is getting a suitable feed.

ROOTS AND APPLES

Root vegetables, such as carrots, swedes, turnips and mangels, are all good for a pony and give variety to his diet. Carrots are particularly popular. Rinse the vegetables first and then cut them into finger-shaped pieces. Avoid round slices as these could stick in a pony's throat and choke him. Apples, both cookers and eaters, should be quartered, core and all. Potatoes are not usually liked by ponies unless they are cooked first. Even then, they may be rejected. Whole turnips and swedes can be left in the field or stable for the pony to nibble at.

SALT

Horses need some salt in their diet, and the easiest way to provide it is to buy a salt block and holder. The holder can be fixed to a fence-post or to the stable wall, so that the pony can lick the block whenever he feels like it. If a grass-kept pony keeps chewing at the bark of a tree or eating soil, it is a sure sign that he is lacking some essential mineral, most probably salt.

TITBITS

Pieces of apple and carrot make the best titbits as they will not harm the pony's teeth. Nevertheless, most ponies like sweet things, especially sugar lumps, and anything minty is very popular. Beware of giving too many titbits to very small ponies as they come to expect something every time anyone appears, and can be bad-tempered if they are not given a present. It is a sensible practice to give small ponies titbits only in a bucket.

FEEDING TIMES

Try to feed your pony at the same time every day. This is most important in winter when ponies are eager for their food and will come to the regular feeding spot as soon as their internal clock tells them that feeding time is near. If several ponies are waiting to be fed, squabbling and kicking may start if you are late.

When ponies are kept in at night in the winter, it is best to put the feeds ready in the individual loose boxes. Where the stables adjoin the field, all you have to do is to open the gate and the ponies will make for their own boxes of their own accord. You can adjust their rugs, if they wear them, while they are eating, and then leave them to finish their meal in peace.

In summer, your pony may be the only one in the field to have a short feed. In this case, take him out of the field to feed him, if possible out of sight of the other ponies.

CHAPTER 12
Essential equipment

When you first owned a pony, the amount of equipment he needed was fairly small: a snaffle bridle, a general-purpose saddle, a head-collar with lead-rope, tack cleaning and grooming kits are usually all that is needed at that stage. Once you start entering competitions regularly, however, or move on to a livelier second pony, you will begin to build up quite a storehouse of bits and pieces. Not all of them can be classed as essential, but there are a number of items which can help you to put up a better performance.

A SECOND SADDLE

Your general-purpose saddle will be perfectly satisfactory for most of the riding you do. However, there are times when a second, specialist saddle can be quite important.

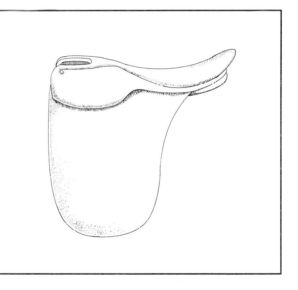

Above Showing saddle, with straight-cut flap.
Left A general purpose saddle.

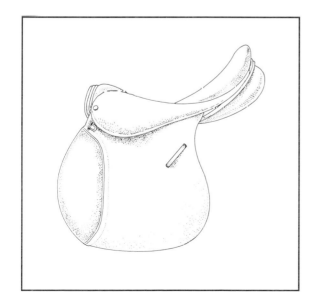

Showing saddle A showing saddle is useful if you intend to show your pony in a big way. The flap is straight-cut, which means that there is not much of it in front of your knee. It is designed to show off your pony's shoulders as well as possible and to avoid any interference when he is demonstrating his fine, flowing, extended trot in front of the judges. It goes without saying that you only use this saddle in the show-ring; it is not suitable for general riding.

Dressage saddle A dressage saddle is similar in appearance to the showing saddle, but it usually has a deeper seat and the bars

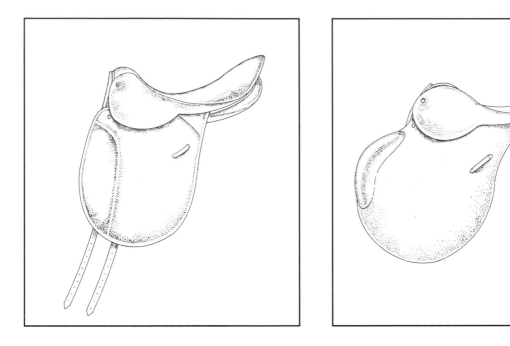

Above left Dressage saddle, with deep seat, short panel and long girth straps.
Above right Jumping saddle, forward cut, with knee rolls.
Opposite A drop noseband, correctly fitted, with the nose-piece high enough not to interfere with the pony's breathing.

are positioned so that each leather hangs down the centre of the flap. The panel is short and the girth straps long. The saddle is designed to place the rider in the dressage position, with the upper thigh almost vertical and the lower leg free. Again, this saddle is intended for the dressage enthusiast, and should not be used for hacking.

Jumping saddle The jumping saddle is very like the general-purpose saddle, except that the flap and panel are more forward-cut and the seat is longer. The effect is to encourage the rider to ride with shorter leathers and to bring her weight over her knees. Very often the forward part of the flap, over the knee rolls, is covered with suede.

If you do acquire a second saddle, for whatever purpose, remember that it should be cleaned regularly to keep it supple and in good condition, even if you use it only on special occasions.

THE BRIDLE

Snaffle bridle For most competitive purposes, a snaffle bridle is best (see page 35). In Pony Club dressage, a snaffle bit is the only type permitted, and some gymkhana organizers ban the use of curb bits of any description. Nevertheless, there are occasions, for

example when out hunting with a strong and lively pony, when you may need more control than a simple jointed snaffle can give you. You can achieve this either by modifying part of the bridle, such as the noseband or the reins, or by switching to a stronger bit.

Double bridle A double bridle is one that has two bits and two pairs of reins. It is used for showing as, in good hands, it reinforces the lessons learned in schooling sessions, resulting in a good natural head carriage and a soft, flexible mouth. A double bridle, however, is not something to be tried out for fun. If you seriously intend to show your pony, you should arrange to have lessons from a competent instructor in the use of a double bridle.

Nosebands

A pony that opens his mouth and crosses his jaw can evade the action of the bit. The answer to this problem is a *drop noseband*, which has a slightly narrower nose-piece than a cavesson does, and is worn below the bit. It is very important to put a drop noseband on correctly because, if the nose-piece is too low, it will interfere with the pony's breathing. The gap between the front of the noseband and the pony's nostrils should be four fingers

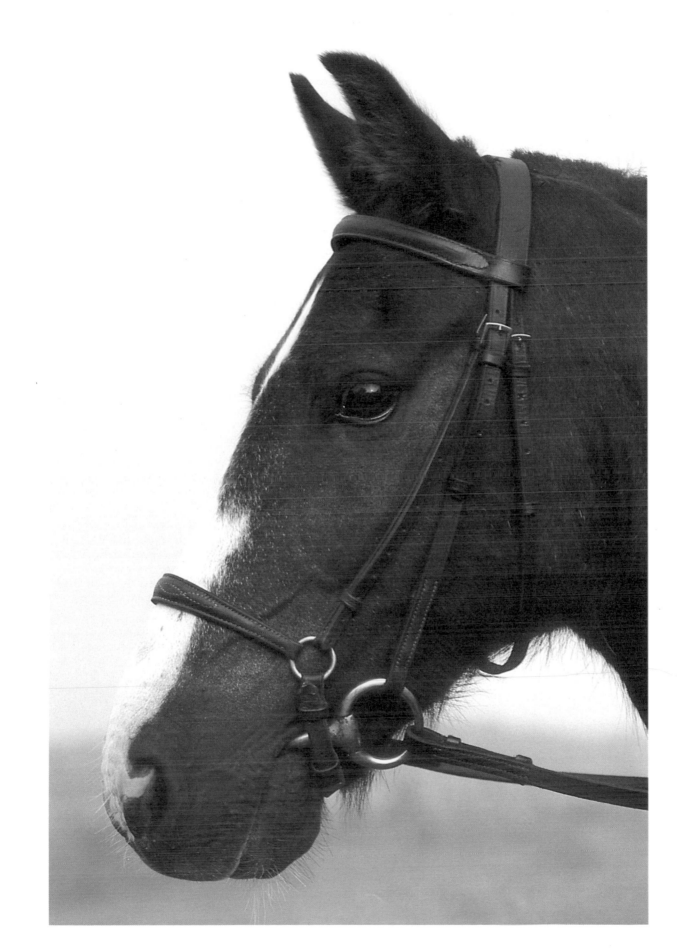

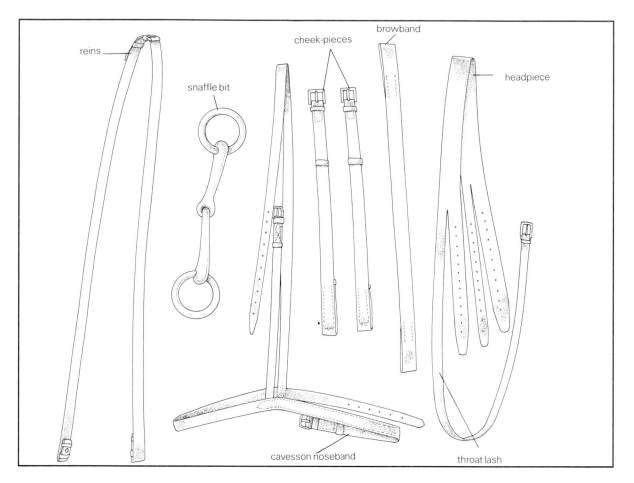

A well-schooled pony should need no more than a plain snaffle bridle; separated into its different parts, **above**, and shown on a pony, **below**.

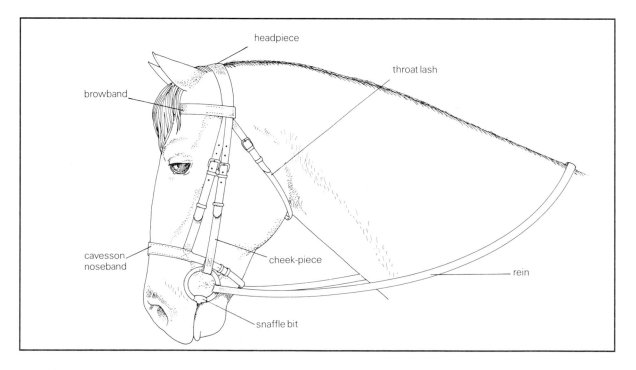

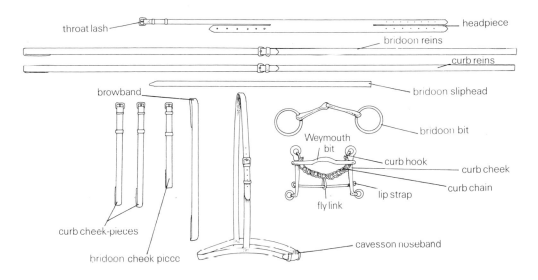

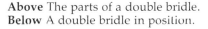

Above The parts of a double bridle.
Below A double bridle in position.

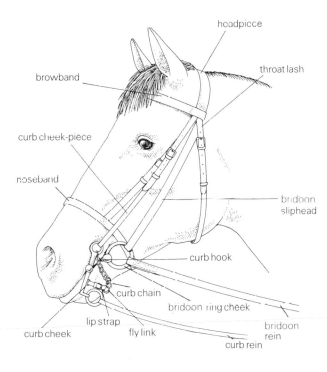

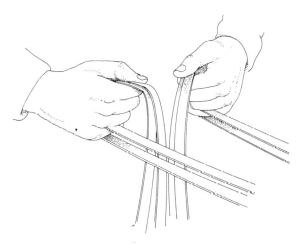

The correct way to hold double reins.

wide with the back resting in the chin groove. It must be tight enough to be effective but not so tight that the pony cannot flex his jaw.

A slightly stronger version of the drop noseband is the *grakle* which has two straps crossing over on the front of the pony's nose and buckled above and below the bit.

If a pony needs both a drop noseband and a standing martingale (see page 100), the *flash* noseband is used. This is a cavesson with a drop noseband attached. The martingale is fixed to the cavesson and not to the drop.

Bits

You should aim to get your pony going well in a snaffle bit. If he resists the bit, this may be due to lack of training – the pony has not yet learned to respond to the signals given to him by his rider; or lack of balance – not unusual in a young pony which is still growing accustomed to the weight of his rider. He may be afraid of the bit, perhaps because it fits badly, or because he has a sore mouth or has had a heavy-handed and unsympathetic rider. In both these cases, it is important for the rider to avoid using force. Patient schooling, under the eye of a competent instructor, should encourage the pony to accept the bit happily, provided that you have made certain that the

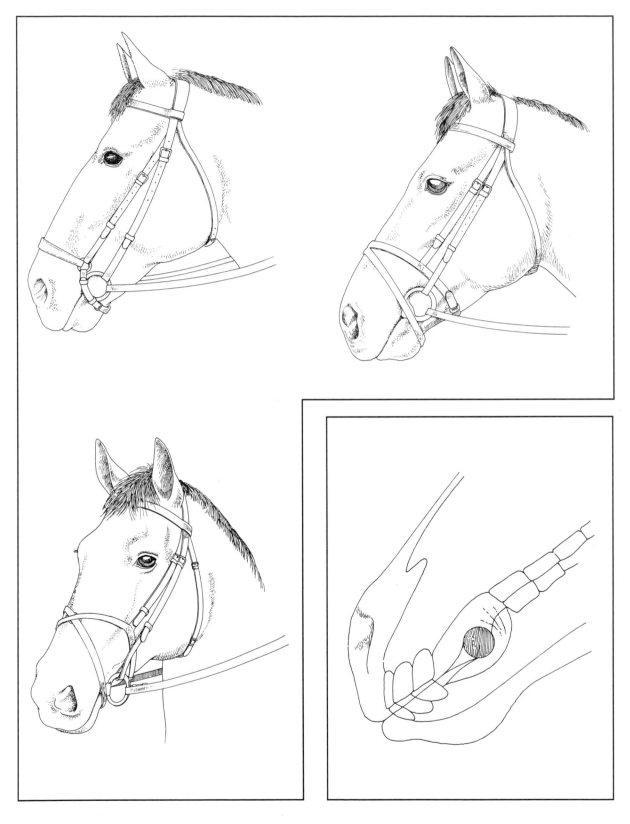

Three nosebands. **Top left** the drop noseband; **top right** the flash; **above** the grackle.

Cross-section of a horse's mouth, showing the gap between the molars and incisor teeth, known as the bars, on which the mouthpiece of the bit bears.

A pony wearing a Pelham bit, fitted with roundings which enable the bit to be used with a single rein.

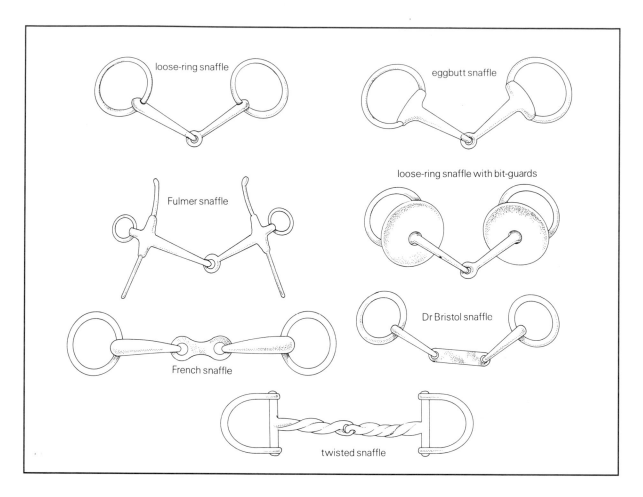

loose-ring snaffle

eggbutt snaffle

Fulmer snaffle

loose-ring snaffle with bit-guards

French snaffle

Dr Bristol snaffle

twisted snaffle

A selection of snaffle bits.

bit is the right size and that he has nothing in his mouth which could be causing him pain.

A bit is the right size if the mouthpiece sticks out on either side about $\frac{1}{2}$ cm ($\frac{1}{4}$ in) when the joint of the snaffle is straight. It is in the correct position in the pony's mouth if it just wrinkles the corners of the lips.

Snaffle bits Snaffle bits come in various designs. The *loose-ring snaffle* has a jointed mouthpiece, and rings that rotate through the holes at either end of the mouthpiece. It is possible for these rings to pinch, and many people prefer to use the *eggbutt snaffle* which has smooth side joints that cannot pinch. Alternatively, a pair of bit-guards can be used to protect the corners of the pony's mouth from soreness. These are rubber discs that fit over each end of the bit between the mouthpiece and the rings.

A *Fulmer snaffle* has extended cheek-pieces which are attached to the bridle's cheek-pieces by leather keepers. These prevent the

bit from rubbing the mouth or being pulled from one side to the other.

Snaffle bits with double joints, such as the *French snaffle* and *Dr Bristol*, are useful on ponies with a narrow tongue groove. The French snaffle has a small rounded central plate between the joints and is fairly mild in its action, but the Dr Bristol with an angled rectangular central plate is a severe bit.

The *twisted snaffle* which has a twisted mouthpiece is a severe bit and should not be necessary on a well-trained pony.

Bits for a double bridle The double bridle has two bits, a jointed snaffle called a bridoon, and a *curb bit*, usually a Weymouth, with a curb chain. It is used by experienced riders to give them precise control, and is only used when the pony is well enough trained to respond positively to the lightest aids.

The Pelham bit This bit combines the qualities of a double bridle into a single mouthpiece. The mouthpiece can be straight

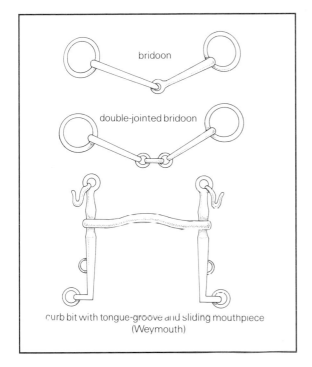

Bits for a double bridle.

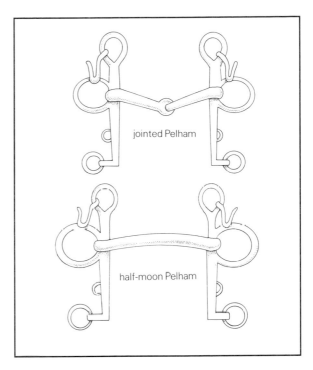

Pelham bits.

or curved, and sometimes has a small arch in the centre; the cheek-pieces are fitted with two pairs of rings and a curb chain. When it is tightened, the curb rein, which is attached to the bottom pair of rings, puts pressure on the poll (the top of the pony's head, between the ears) and, through the curb chain, on the chin groove. The top rein acts on the lips, corners of the mouth, tongue and roof of the mouth.

Those who find it difficult to ride with two reins sometimes use a Pelham bit fitted with roundings. These are leather pieces which are attached to the bridoon and curb rings on the bit and enable a single rein to be used.

Although some ponies do seem to go well in a Pelham bit, on the whole it is better to use a snaffle in conjunction with a drop noseband if greater control is needed.

Decoration on bridles

A coloured browband is permissible in all classes except showing events. This is usually made from leather and covered in a shark's tooth pattern of strips of plastic or velvet in contrasting colours. The disadvantage of such a browband is that it is not possible to get at the leather core to oil it and keep it supple. Velvet covered browbands are difficult to

clean, but the plastic-covered type just need a wipe over to keep them bright.

Showing browbands may be plain leather or brass-mounted. The brass mounts or studs should be polished. These browbands, however, are not allowed in official Pony Club mounted games competitions.

The noseband may be plain leather or have a stitched pattern on the front part. Both are cleaned in the normal way with saddle soap or leather dressing.

Reins

Narrow reins are often used for showing, but slightly wider reins give a better grip to the hands. Reins of plaited leather, or those covered with rubber, are easier to grip in wet weather. Always measure the reins before buying a new pair, as long reins on a short-necked pony will give too much surplus. The loop will hang so far down that it can catch your foot. Many children, especially when taking part in gymkhana events in which a short rein is necessary, shorten the rein by tying a loose knot in it. Remember to undo the knot before putting the bridle away, or the leather could become damaged or cracked where the knot is tied.

ADDITIONAL TACK

Martingales

Standing martingale One of the commonest problems with a headstrong pony is the habit of throwing up the head in an effort to evade the restrictions imposed by your hands. Once a pony's head gets above a certain point, the action of the bit becomes much less effective, and if your riding is not yet advanced enough to bring his head down through the use of your seat and legs, then some extra control is needed. The use of a standing martingale stops the pony from carrying or tossing his head too high. It consists of a strap with a loop at each end; one end is attached to the underside of a cavesson noseband and the other to the girth. The strap passes between the pony's forelegs, and is supported by a neck-strap.

Running martingale.

Standing martingale.

To be sure that a standing martingale is correctly fitted, hold the horse's head in the right position and push the strap upwards with your hand. It should touch the pony's throat. The strap is fitted with buckles to enable adjustments to be made.

Running martingale In this form of martingale, one end is attached to the girth, and it is supported by a neck-strap. The front part of the strap, however, divides into two, and each end finishes in a ring, through which the reins pass. The purpose of this type of martingale is to ensure that pressure via the reins on to the bit always comes from the right direction, however much the rider may throw her hands about. To fit the running martingale, attach one end to the girth and check that the rings on the other end reach to the pony's throat. Rubber stops should be attached to the reins to prevent the rings from sliding down and getting hooked over the stud billets or buckles where rein and bit rings meet.

Irish martingale This is a short strap about 10 cm (4 in) long, with a ring at either end, which links the two sides of the pair of reins underneath the pony's neck. Its purpose is to prevent the reins from going over the pony's head.

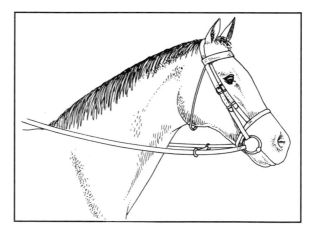

Irish martingale.

Properly fitted running martingale. When the pony's head is in the normal position, as here, the martingale does not interfere with the head carriage. It comes into play only if the pony throws up his head.

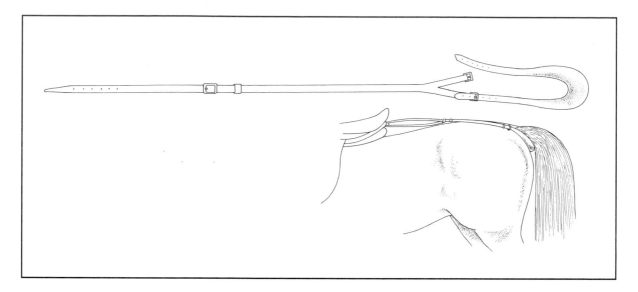

The parts of a crupper, **top**, and in position, **below**.

Breastplate and crupper

Some ponies have flat, low withers, others high, prominent withers: both can make it difficult to keep a saddle in the right place.

If your pony's withers are low, you may find that the saddle tends to slip forwards while you are riding. The remedy could lie in having the saddle re-stuffed and you should consult a reputable saddler on this point. If, however, re-stuffing does not help the answer may be to fit a *crupper*. This is a strap with a padded loop at one end through which the tail passes. The other end fastens to a D-ring on the back of the saddle.

If, on the other hand, the saddle tends to slip back, a *breastplate* will hold it in position. This consists of a neck-strap which is connected to metal D-rings on the front of each side of the saddle by means of two short straps on either side of the pony's neck. A broader strap passing between the pony's forelegs connects the neck-strap to the girth. An alternative to this is the *breast-girth*. This consists of a wide webbing strap which is fastened to the girth straps under the saddle flaps. A short connecting strap over the neck in front of the withers holds the breast-girth horizontally across the pony's chest.

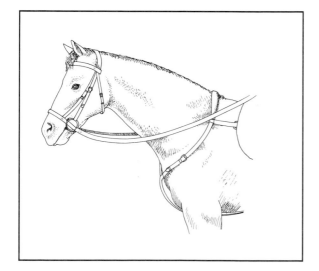

Breastplate.

Breast-girth.

Numnah

This is a saddle-shaped pad which is worn under the saddle to protect the back, either when the pony is being ridden for a long period, or as a temporary measure with a saddle that needs re-stuffing. It can be made from a number of different materials, including sheepskin, which is expensive, felt and sorbo-rubber. Some numnahs are quilted. The best sort is made from natural fibres, which are absorbent and do not cause sweating and inflammation. The numnah can be fastened to the saddle by means of straps which pass round the girth straps.

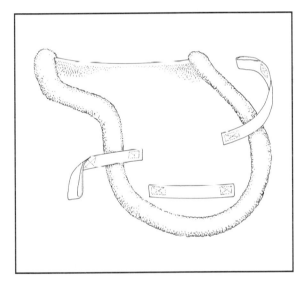

Numnah.

HORSE CLOTHING

Once you start entering competitions regularly and taking your pony to shows in a trailer or horse-box, he will need various forms of protective clothing.

Types of rug

There are many types of rug (called blankets in the USA), each having a different purpose. The decision on which type to buy first can be a difficult one, assuming that you cannot afford to buy three or four at once. And it will be influenced by the time of year when you buy it, as your pony's needs in summer are different from those in the winter. When visiting agricultural or major horse shows, take time to look round the trade stands; it is often possible to pick up a bargain or special show offer, and with so many suppliers gathered together in a small area, you can study and compare prices and quality.

Make certain that you know your pony's measurements. Most rugs are sold in sizes ranging from 1.2 m or 1.3 m to 1.8 m or 2 m (4 ft or 4 ft 6 in to 6 ft or 6 ft 6 in). This measurement represents the length of the pony from a point in the centre of the chest, where the rug's buckles would lie, to a point on the pony's quarters vertically below the root of the tail. Other measurements, such as the depth of the rug and the length along the back, are proportional to the first measurement, so you need only the one measurement to assess the size of rug to buy.

Some rugs are sold with their own surcingle. With others, you have to buy a surcingle or roller separately. Always check whether it is included in the price.

Anti-sweat rugs As a start, an anti-sweat rug is the most useful type. It is made of open cotton mesh and is used on an overheated pony to help him to cool down without catching cold. It can be used on its own or under a second rug, which should be made from natural material. Anti-sweat rugs are usually sold in three sizes: small, medium and large. Because it is rather shapeless, it is better to be too small than too big. It washes easily.

Summer sheets A summer sheet is made of cotton, often in a checked design, and should be supplied with a matching surcingle and fillet-string. It is used to protect a groomed pony from dust and flies, and when travelling in warm weather. The fillet-string is usually a plaited string which is tied to one side of the back edge of the sheet; it passes loosely under the tail and fastens to the other side. Its purpose is to prevent the sheet from blowing in the wind.

Day rugs These are made of wool, usually in a dark colour with a contrasting binding. A day rug will keep a clipped and stabled pony warm when he is standing in his box during the day. The day rug can also be used for travelling.

Night rugs A night rug is worn by a stabled, clipped pony during the night. It is made of jute, often lined with wool. It can, of course, also be used during the day, but, because it tends to get dirty when the pony lies down, it is usually kept for night wear only. It may be supplied with a stitched-on

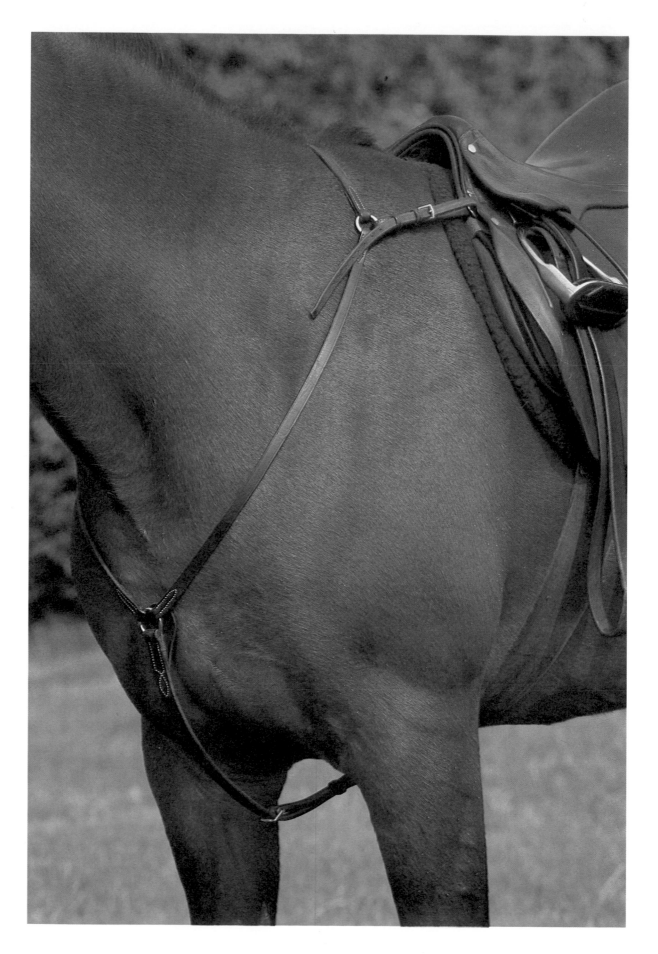

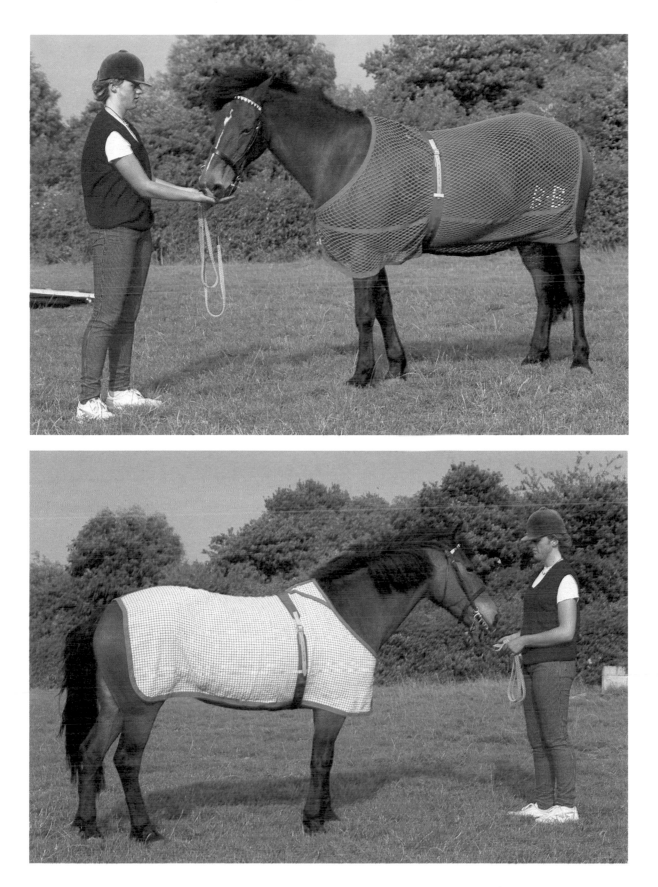

Left A breastplate, used to prevent the saddle from slipping back. **Top** An anti-sweat sheet. The open mesh allows the pony to cool down without getting cold. **Above** The same pony in a summer sheet. This light cotton rug protects the pony from dust and flies.

surcingle, but to avoid unnecessary pressure on the pony's spine the surcingle should be cut off, and a separate roller used instead.

All-purpose rugs These are made of quilted material, usually man-made. An all-purpose rug can be worn by a stabled pony day or night and is easy to keep clean because it can be put in the washing-machine. However, man-made fibres do not breathe, unlike wool or cotton, and can make horses sweat if the weather is mild. It is a very good type of rug for travelling.

In very cold weather, the clipped, stabled pony may need extra warmth during the night. For this purpose, blankets made of wool or acrylic are used and are put on under the night rug.

Exercise rugs This is a short rug, often striped, which covers the horse's loins and quarters when he is being ridden out at exercise. They are mostly used by racehorses. A hardy pony does not usually need an exercise rug even if he is clipped right out and stabled. However, a *waterproof sheet* can be extremely useful, even on a pony normally kept at grass. It protects the pony's back and loins when he is being ridden in very wet weather. The back of the sheet is shaped to fit over the pony's quarters.

New Zealand rugs A New Zealand rug is designed to stay in position on a pony that is loose in a field, even when he rolls. There are, in fact, many different designs, but they all have the same purpose. Some are retained by one or two surcingles or rollers and a system of cross-over straps which pass between the pony's hind legs. Others have diagonal surcingles. Yet others rely on the cut of the rug and judiciously placed tucks to conform to the contours of the pony's body, to prevent it from slipping. A New Zealand rug is unnecessary on an unclipped pony, but they are useful on a clipped pony to replace the protection that his coat would have given him if he had not been clipped.

The disadvantage of a New Zealand rug is that it can chafe, particularly on the points of the shoulder, around the withers and between the hind legs. A pony in a New Zealand rug *must* be caught up and inspected twice daily to make adjustments and reduce the chances of chafing to a minimum.

Rollers and surcingles These are both straps which pass round the pony's belly, just behind the withers, and are fastened by

Rear view of New Zealand rug, showing how cross-over leg straps help to keep it in place.

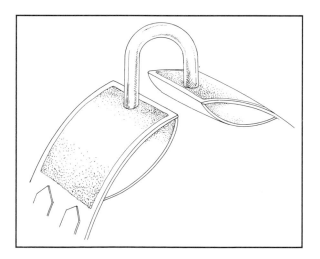

An anti-cast roller.

buckles to hold the rug in place. The difference between them is that the roller is fitted on the underside with pads, which rest on either side of the pony's spine and prevent pressure on the spine.

A *roller pad* is a thick piece of foam rubber which is placed under the surcingle to reduce pressure on the spine. The pad should be wider than the surcingle.

An *anti-cast roller* is made with a projecting bar of metal on the upper part of the roller, above the padded section. It is worn by a stabled horse and stops him from going right over when he rolls, which might cause him to get jammed (cast) against the stable wall. It should not be necessary in a big loose box.

Putting on a rug

Drape the rug over your arm; then with both hands toss it well forward over the pony's withers. Straighten out the front and fasten the chest buckle. Move to the pony's quarters and pull the rug back, again using both hands. As long as your pony does not kick, move behind him and check that the rug is straight and level. Put the roller or surcingle in place, making certain that the end with the buckle passes under the belly. Place the roller pad in position and do up the roller. It should be firm but not too tight. Remove wrinkles in the rug by running your fingers between roller and rug on both sides. Make certain that there is no drag on the shoulders. The roller should lie in the same place as the girth on a saddle, just behind the elbow.

If a blanket is being used, this goes under the rug and should be adjusted to ensure that the back end of the blanket is level with the edge of the rug. Any surplus blanket at the neck end is folded back after the roller or surcingle has been fastened.

Removing a rug

Undo and remove the roller or surcingle. Undo the chest buckle. Fold the front part of the rug over the back. Grip the centre front with your left hand and the centre back with your right and sweep the rug off over the quarters in one movement. When a blanket has been used, both blanket and rug are taken off at the same time. Shake the rug and blanket outside, fold up and place them in a safe dry place, clear of the ground. Always keep a rug and its surcingle together.

Protection while travelling

Although partitions in a trailer or horse-box may be padded, and the floor covered with a thick bed of straw or shavings, a pony can easily bang himself if he is caught off-balance by the vehicle's movements. To minimize the risk of injury, it is sensible to give him as much protection as possible.

Many ponies, even those which are good travellers, sweat with anticipation or excitement when they are in the confines of a trailer. To be sure that he arrives in good

The position of a blanket when worn under a rug. **Left** The blanket is put on first, well forward up the neck, and the front corners are folded up so that they lie on the neck. **Right** The rug is put on over the blanket, and the corners of the blanket are folded back and secured under the roller.

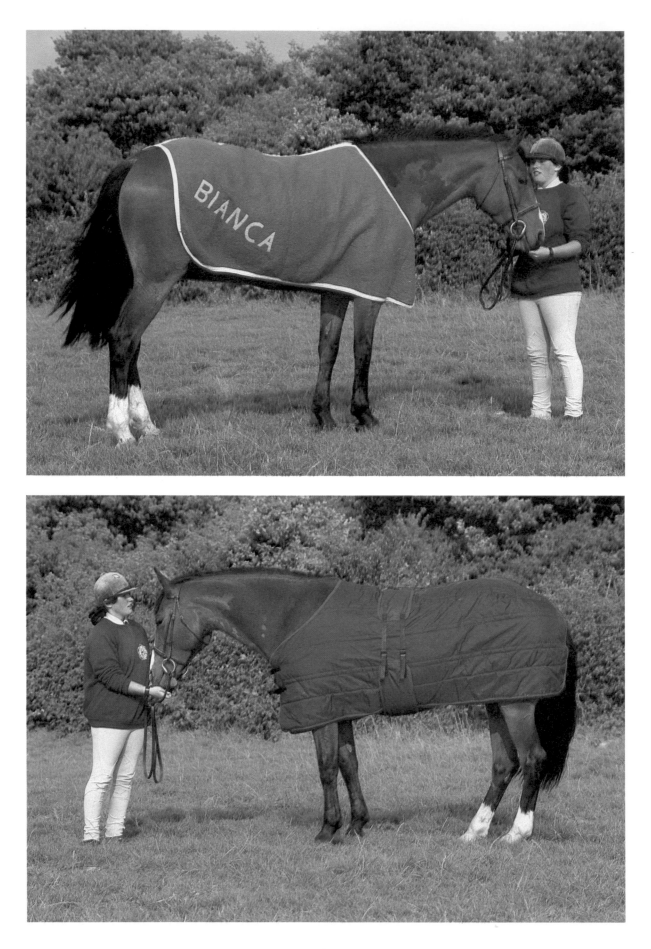

condition, put him in an anti-sweat rug, with or without a sheet or day rug on top. The front of the day rug can be folded back and tucked flat under the roller or surcingle. A pony should never travel in a rug without a roller to keep it in place, as the rug might slip off during the journey and cause the pony to panic.

Stable bandages or *travelling boots* will protect the pony's legs. Travelling boots are made from fleece-lined rectangular pieces of leather, plastic or canvas. They fasten round the leg and come well down over the coronet. They are held in place by straps with Velcro fastenings, and are quick and easy to put on and remove.

Knee caps and *hock boots* may be used if necessary to guard against injury to the leg joints. A *poll pad* will protect the top of the

pony's head if he is nervy and therefore likely to throw up his head when he is moving into or out of a trailer.

A *tail bandage* (see page 62) is needed to protect the tail if it gets rubbed against the closed-up trailer ramp. It can be covered in addition by a *tail guard*: a wedge-shaped piece of material that fastens with tapes round the tail, and is attached by tapes at the pointed end to the surcingle.

Bandages

Stable bandages These are designed to keep legs warm, and to help legs which have become wet during a ride to dry off, therefore reducing the risk of chapping. They are made of wool or stockinette and are usually available in sets of four. They should be put on tight enough to stop them from slipping but

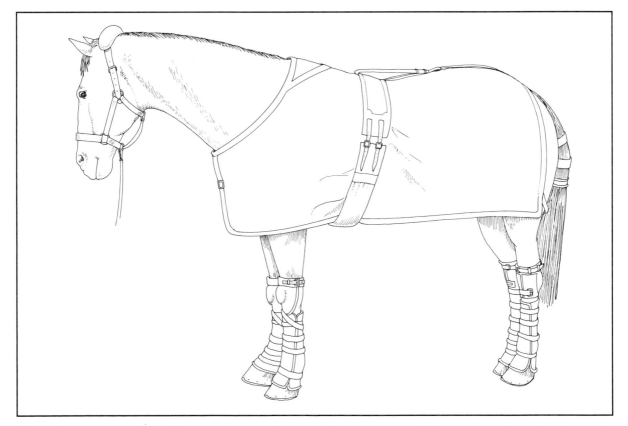

Above Ready for travelling. The pony wears a day rug, with surcingle and fillet string, poll guard, tail guard, knee caps, hock boots and travelling boots.
Pages 108–9 Top left Day rug made of wool and bound with a contrasting colour. **Bottom left** Quilted all-purpose rug with its own attached surcingle. This type of rug, which washes easily, may be used for night or day wear. **Top right** New Zealand rug of the right size for this pony. It protects the back and loins but is not too long to interfere with the pony's movements. **Bottom right** Ready for travelling. The pony wears a summer sheet, fleecy leg guards which reach to the coronet and a tail guard over his tail bandage.

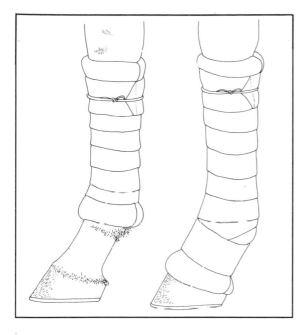

Bandages in position. **Left** Exercise bandage; **right** stable bandage.

not so tight that they cause marks or lumps on the leg. If *gamgee* is used underneath the bandages, this will help to prevent damage to the legs.

A leg should be bandaged downwards from just below the knee. Stable bandages cover the fetlock and reach to the coronet. Start by holding the free end of the bandage against the leg and take a turn round the leg to hold the end in place, fold the free end down, secure it with the next turn of the bandage, and continue down the leg to the coronet. Now bandage upwards until you are back where you started, by which time you should have come to the end of the bandage. Fasten off, either by tying the tapes in a bow or using the clips or Velcro provided. The knot should lie on the outside of the leg, but not on the front or back where it could press on the bone or tendon.

Exercise bandages These are made of an elasticated material, and are designed to give support to the legs while the pony is working. For this reason an exercise bandage stretches from just below the knee to just above the fetlock joint. Gamgee, cotton wool or foam rubber should be wrapped round the leg, and should be completely flat; the bandage is put on over it. Gamgee that protrudes at either end can be trimmed with scissors. The exer-

cise bandage is put on in the same way as the stable bandage except that the upward bandaging begins just above the fetlock joint. Fasten the tapes on the outside of the leg, and for extra security, wrap a band of insulating tape round the leg, over the knot.

Protective boots
Injuries to legs can be caused by bad conformation, poor shoeing, bad riding, inexperience (especially in a young horse), tiredness or an accident. The latter two most commonly occur in competitive riding, especially cross-country. The former can, hopefully, be prevented by good schooling, careful choice of farrier, or the genuine desire on the part of the rider to improve.

In all cases, however, some protection can be given to the pony by using one or other of the various types of protective boots available.

Overreach boots These are bell-shaped and made of rubber. They fit round the lower part of the pastern to protect the heels of the front feet, especially the bulbs of the heels, from damage caused by overreaching. It is caused by the toe of the rear foot striking or

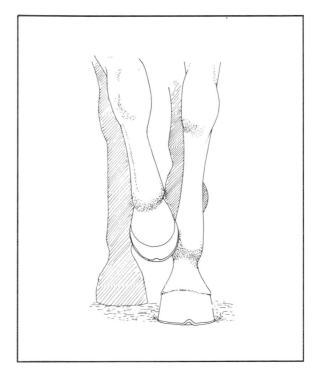

Brushing. The inside of one hoof is interfering with the opposite leg, which can cause injury. Brushing boots will prevent the pony injuring himself by this habit.

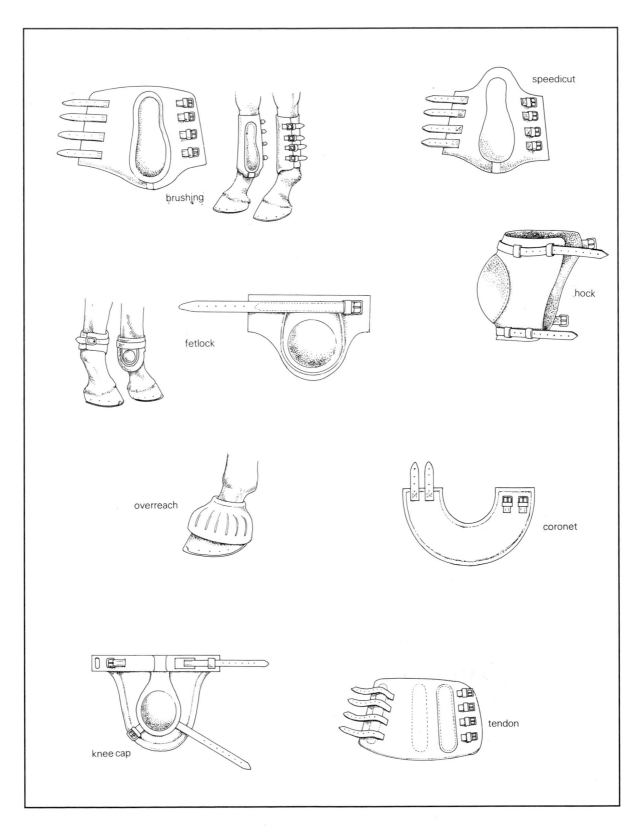

Protective boots.

Useful precautions to take when the pony is jumping. Support bandages over gamgee protect the tendons. The red band of insulating tape ensures that the knotted tapes will not come undone. Bell-shaped overreach boots protect the heels, which may get knocked by the hind feet if the pony is tired or galloping over rough ground.

treading on the heel of the front. It is usually an accidental injury, which can happen while galloping or jumping, particularly in soft ground.

Brushing boots These protect the inside of the leg from injury caused by a blow from the opposite foot. Careful shoeing may help to prevent brushing if it is caused by bad conformation. Made of felt and leather, they have extra padding on the part which covers the inside of the leg, and are fastened on the outside by four or five straps or Velcro fasteners. Ordinary brushing boots protect the fetlock joint and the part of the leg above it almost as far as the knee. *Fetlock boots,* *Yorkshire boots* and *rubber rings* protect only the fetlock joint.

Speedicut boots These are similar to brushing boots but are worn higher up the leg and protect the inside of the knee joint from injury by the opposite foot. Speedicutting is more dangerous and the wounds usually more severe than those caused by brushing.

Coronet boots These protect the coronet region from being trodden on by other ponies. For this reason they are often used on horses travelling in company.

Tendon boots These have padding at the rear of the leg and protect the tendons from a high overreach.

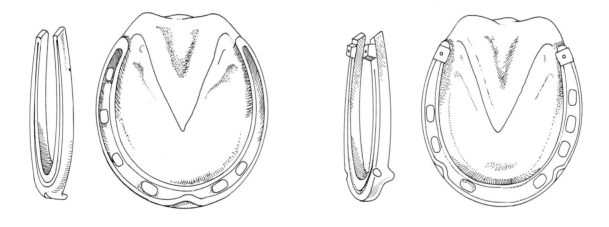

Left: A front shoe with a feathered edge. This shoe will help to correct faults, such as brusing, that are due to weak conformation.
Right: Hind shoe fitted with studs. Studs are used to give a pony better grip when he is jumping or competing in gymkhanas on slippery ground.

CHAPTER 13
Schooling and jumping

The secret of good, sympathetic riding lies in achieving balance and harmony. You must aim to remain in perfect balance with your pony's movements, not only at each of the different paces, but also during transitions (the changes from one pace to another). This will enable you to give clear instructions to the pony (through the use of the aids) and will enable the pony to respond to them correctly, thereby keeping you and the pony in harmony.

BALANCE

When you first learned to ride, your instructor will have stressed the importance of sitting 'square', with your hips parallel to the pony's quarters and your shoulders parallel to his shoulders, while you keep looking

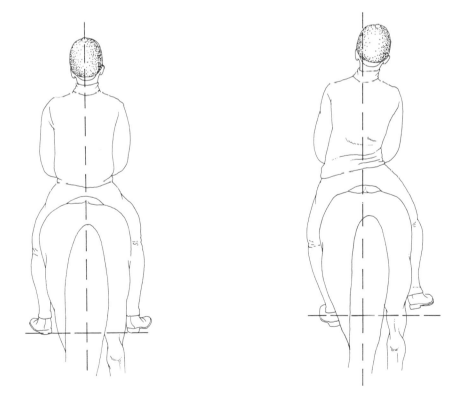

A square seat is one of the first requisites of a balanced seat. If your seat is crooked, **right**, the pony cannot balance himself properly with the weight of his rider.

ahead in the direction in which you are going. In this position you remain balanced on the pony.

The pony also has to learn how to balance himself, when carrying the weight of a rider. He must use his muscles correctly: his weight should be on his hind legs, he should carry his head and neck in a natural position, and give no resistance to the bit.

The rider must create forward movement, called *impulsion*, through the use of the lower leg and seat (see page 117). This gives the impression of energy even at a walk. There must be no sign of the pony dragging his feet. He should be alert and supple, his hind legs active and his paces rhythmic.

Three diagrams showing how the rider's position has to change with the pony's paces in order to keep the rider's centre of gravity in balance with the pony's. **Top left**, at a walk; **top right**, at a gallop; **bottom**, jumping.

THE AIDS

These are the means by which the rider tells the pony what to do. They should always be clear and should only be repeated if the pony does not respond immediately. There are two kinds of aids. The voice, body, legs and hands are *natural aids.* Whips and spurs are *artificial aids.* Artificial aids are used only to emphasize the natural aids.

The voice The voice encourages, calms, praises and occasionally scolds the pony. With a young or unschooled pony, the voice can be used to instruct. Phrases like 'walk on', 'halt', 'trot' or 'steady' will help to reinforce the signals given by the legs or hands. The voice, however, should not be used during a dressage test.

The body This can pass information to the pony by its movement; in addition the muscles of the seat help to create impulsion. The rider, however, should always remain in balance.

The legs While the thigh muscles stay relaxed and the hip and knee joints stay supple, the lower part of the leg is used to

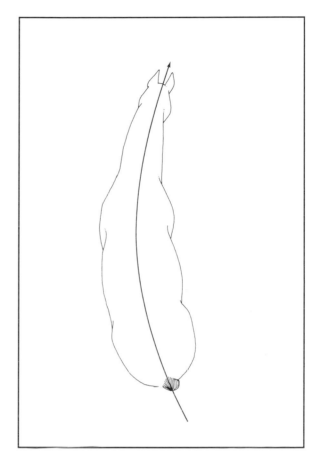

A pony is said to be bending correctly when his body follows the direction of the curve and his hind feet follow the tracks of the front feet.

Aids to turning the pony. **Left** The rider's hand is brought sideways and forwards, leading the pony in a wide arc. **Right** The rider's legs and seat control forward movement and the hindquarters while pressure on the inside rein shows the pony which way to go.

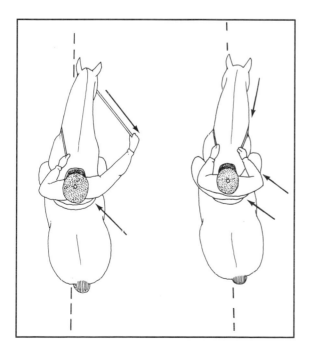

give definite signals. A short, sharp application of pressure by the inside leg asks for impulsion. Increased pressure on one side makes the pony bend correctly when moving in a circle or curve. A correct bend occurs when the pony's body follows the line of the curve without deviating or bending away from it.

The hindquarters are controlled by the outside lower leg. Pressure behind the girth, quickly but firmly applied, with the leg returning immediately to its normal position, asks the pony to canter. Continuous pressure controls the direction of the hindquarters and should cease once the movement has been correctly carried out.

The hands The hands indicate direction and control the pony's speed. Quick pressure of the inside hand, followed by relaxation of the fingers indicates direction. The outside hand repeats this movement to regulate the pace.

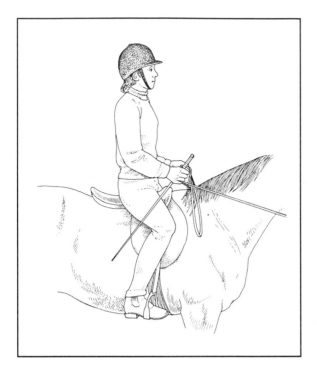

The correct way to carry a whip.

The whip used to reinforce a leg aid.

The whip This is brought into action only if the pony does not obey the leg aids. It should be used sharply once and your hand must be removed from the rein as you apply the whip to avoid confusing your pony. The whip should be applied just behind the leg that gave the aid.

A standard whip measures 74 cm (30 in) in length. When schooling a longer whip 91 cm (3 ft) may be used, without taking the hand from the rein.

Spurs Blunt spurs – that is, spurs without rowels – are the only acceptable type of spurs. They are worn with the necks pointing down-

A spur correctly fitted.

wards and the arm of the spur parallel with the sole of the boot. The buckles always fasten on the outside of the boot. To use a spur correctly, you should turn your toe slightly outwards so that the side of the spur neck touches the pony's side. If you turn your foot out too far, the back of the spur will dig into the pony and this is incorrect. Spurs should only be worn by experienced riders.

SCHOOLING

Schooling is the means by which rider and pony together achieve *harmony* and *balance*.

Flatwork This is the term given to school-ing work performed in an arena, or manege. Flatwork covers work at the different paces, and changes of pace and direction. Circles and turns are used to encourage the pony to bend his body correctly. It helps to build up the rider's feel for the horse, so that she learns to know without having to ask a spectator whether her mount's outline and pace are right.

A common fault among inexperienced riders, for example, is that they do not know, without looking down, whether the pony is leading with the correct leg at the canter. You should be able to feel which shoulder is slightly ahead of the other and which hind leg reaches the ground first.

Hillwork The best way of improving a pony's balance is to ride up and down hills. The slope of the ground encourages him to get his weight off the forehand and builds up the muscles in his quarters. He also learns to use his hocks actively. In addition, this type of work is an excellent preliminary to jumping.

Effective schooling requires an understanding of the correct use of the aids.

USE OF THE AIDS

For the walk

When you ask a pony to move forward from a halt into a walk, you do so with your lower legs: a quick application of pressure on the pony's sides, followed by the give and take of your hands to correspond with the movements of the pony's head. When the walk is proceeding at a calm yet active pace, the hind leg should reach the ground in front of the print left by the foreleg on the same side. Occasionally, let the pony walk on a loose rein (which is how you should leave a dressage arena after you have completed a test). Allow the reins to slip through your fingers so that they become completely slack, while the pony stretches his head and neck.

The rider's position at the walk.

For the trot

Similar but slightly stronger aids are used to urge your pony into a trot, either from a halt or from a walk. Your legs and seat create impulsion, while your hands give sufficiently so as not to restrict the forward movement. You start to rise as the pony settles into the rhythm of the pace.

From time to time, change the diagonal. At the trot you rise when one diagonal pair of legs touches the ground and sit down on the other. If you sit for two beats, you change the diagonal that you rise on. It is more comfortable for your pony if you do this every so often.

An extended trot.

It is also a good idea to carry out a few movements at the sitting trot, consciously pushing your seat bones well into the saddle and trying not to bump. However, never continue at a sitting trot for too long as it can be very tiring.

For the canter

Prepare for the canter a few strides in advance of asking your pony to change his pace, and always see that the preceding pace is moving ahead with plenty of balance and impulsion. Sit down to the trot and indicate the direction of the canter by feeling the pony's mouth with the inside hand. Keep your inside leg on the pony's girth, but move your outside leg back a little so that you can apply pressure strongly and definitely to the pony's side behind the girth. If you have given the aids correctly and the pony responds properly, he should strike off into a true canter with his inside legs leading.

Many ponies favour one side more than the other. That is to say, if asked to canter in a straight line, they will always lead off with either the near side or off side legs. If you ride your pony in a circle with his favoured side

The transition from trot to canter, working on a curve. The pony collects himself to lead off with the correct – i.e., the inside – leg.

When a pony leads on the wrong – outside – leg at the canter, he is unbalanced. The rider should bring him back to the trot and give the correct aids.

on the inside, you will have no problems getting him to lead off correctly. Trouble arises when you ride round on the other rein (that is, in the other direction). To be in balance, he must lead with the other legs, which he may not want to do.

A pony which canters a circle with the outside legs leading is said to be cantering false or counter-leading. Sometimes, perhaps because you have given the wrong aids or he has misunderstood them, the pony will canter disunited. This means that his leading hind leg is on the opposite side to his leading foreleg.

If the strike-off is wrong, it must be corrected immediately by bringing the pony back to a trot and moving into a canter again. Flying changes, when a pony changes the leading legs without going out of a canter, should not be attempted until you and the pony are very experienced. Nevertheless, many ponies, especially those with natural balance and impulsion, will change legs instinctively to match changes of direction. You have only to watch a skilful little gymkhana pony as he nips in and out of bending poles to see this.

For the gallop
Use the aid for increased impulsion and take up the galloping position, with your weight forward on your knees and stirrups and your seat just out of the saddle. Shorten the reins slightly to maintain contact with the mouth.

For decreases in pace
Use quickly-applied pressure of the outside hand to slow the pony down, while your legs continue to supply impulsion. Make certain that the pony remains balanced and on the bit.

For the halt
The aids here are the same as for decreases in pace. It is important that your legs should stay in contact with the pony's sides as he stops, to avoid loss of impulsion and to

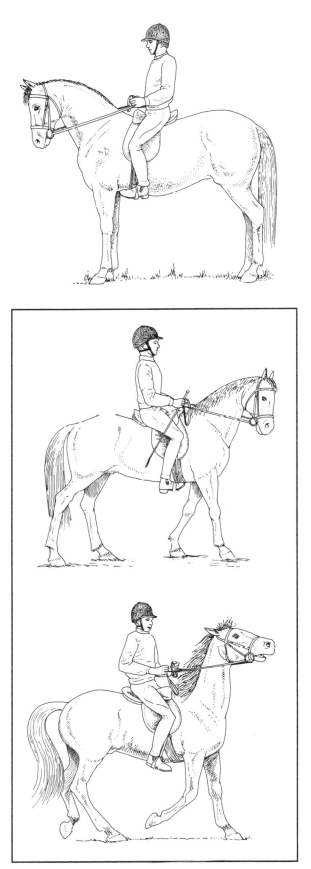

Top right A smooth halt with pony and rider nicely balanced.

Reining back. **Above right** The correct way. **Right** The wrong way.

prevent the tendency for him to step back. The halt should be square and straight, with the pony's weight spread evenly over his four legs.

For the rein back

It is quite difficult for a pony to walk backwards correctly without loss of balance. If his head goes up and his back hollows, he is unbalanced and resistant, and more schooling is needed in the forward paces. The aids for the rein back may seem contradictory to the pony because the rider's legs ask him to go forward while the hands hold him back. Lessons in the rein back should always be carried out quietly. You should never try to make him walk back too far – one step or two is sufficient at the beginning. As soon as he has stepped back the required number of strides, ask him to go forward again immediately, using the correct leg aid and giving with your hands.

JUMPING

The object of the rider when going over a jump is to give the pony as much help as possible by keeping the weight in the correct position at each phase. At the same time, you should relax and concentrate on maintaining good balance, impulsion and rhythm.

Allow the pony to choose the moment of take-off until you have learnt to judge it accurately yourself. Aim at going with him, and interfere as little as possible.

There are five phases to the jump, whether you are tackling knock-down fences in the show-ring or fixed fences on a cross-country course.

Phase one is the *approach*. The pony must be going forward with balance, impulsion and rhythm. Phase two is the *take-off*. As the pony approaches the jump, he lowers his head and stretches his neck, gathering himself for the moment of take-off. Energy for the spring comes from his hocks and his whole body foreshortens: his head comes up, his neck shortens and he lifts himself off the ground, folding his forelegs under him. Phase three is the *moment of suspension*. This is the moment when he is in mid-air. His legs are tucked up under him, his head and neck stretch forwards and downwards to their fullest extent. His back should be rounded, forming a 'bascule'. Phase four is the *landing*. As the pony approaches the ground, he braces his forelegs and raises his head and neck to keep his balance and to be ready to move away as soon as his hind legs hit the ground. The final phase is the *recovery*. This is the first stride after landing, and the start of the approach to the next jump. His hocks should be well under him in order to regain balance, impulsion and rhythm.

The rider's position

You must make certain that your weight is over the pony's centre of gravity at the take-off and during the moment of suspension, returning to the upright position on landing. This is done by bending forward at the hips – not the waist. It is easier to support this movement if your stirrup-leathers are shortened, making the angles formed by the knee and ankle joints more acute. You should be able to take and hold the jumping position at both the trot and the canter, showing that you have a balanced, independent seat, and that you do not have to hang on to the reins or rest your hands on the pony's neck in order to maintain it. You must be able to give with the

The five phases of the jump. **From left**: the approach; the take-off; the moment of suspension; the landing; and the recovery.

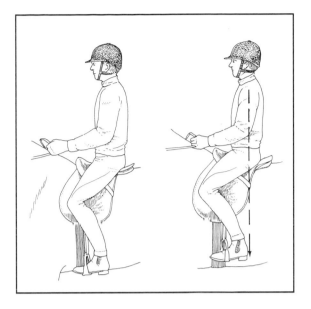

Stirrup-leathers should be shortened for jumping. **Left** The length for riding on the flat. **Right** Jumping length.

The jumping position. The rider is balanced, without resting on the hands.

hands, following the movement of the pony's head and neck, while you are jumping.

At the approach You should sit lightly in the saddle without interfering with the pony's balance and impulsion. Your lower legs rest against the pony's side and your hands keep a gentle but steady contact with the pony's mouth.

At take-off and moment of suspension Fold forward at the hips, keeping your back flat and your head up, looking ahead. Never be tempted to look down at the jump, or lean to one side, or your weight will be unevenly distributed and the pony will have a harder job to keep his rhythm. Your heels should be well down, joints supple, and your lower leg should not slip back. Your hands continue to keep a light contact with the pony's mouth and to give with the movement of head and neck.

At landing and recovery Your body moves back into the upright position, and your leg lightly touches the pony's side ready to get him into his stride for the next approach, while your eyes look towards the next jump.

Points to remember
* Practise the fold forward from the hips at trot and canter.

* Beware of throwing your hands up the pony's neck, so that contact between your fingers and the pony's mouth is lost. This is a common fault with beginners, often caused by fear of being left behind, and it produces inadvertent jabbing at the pony's mouth. The sudden loss of contact may confuse the pony and eventually lead to his refusing.
* Consciously keep your lower leg in the right position, with the heels down.
* Never fiddle with the reins or flap your legs wildly.
* Keep your shoulders soft and flexible.
* Keep your back straight.
* Keep your head up and look straight in front of you.

Schooling over trotting poles
Trotting poles are beneficial schooling aids to both pony and rider. This type of schooling helps a pony to learn obedience and to develop balance, rhythm and co-ordination. It also encourages him to lower his head and neck, to round his back and engage his hocks. It helps the rider to develop balance, rhythm and timing, and teaches her how to judge distance and placing.

Jumping poles may be used as trotting poles. They are set parallel to each other on

Trotting poles should be used to improve the pony's balance.

the ground, between 1.2 and 1.5 m (4 and 5 ft) apart, depending on the size of the pony. A minimum of three poles should be used, and they should be pegged to the ground to prevent them from rolling about.

Always take trotting poles at a rising trot. If possible, ask someone else to watch whether each footfall is exactly in the centre of the space between the poles. It is very important that the rider should not look down. You must look up and forwards, otherwise the pony could become unbalanced.

When your pony is working confidently and correctly over trotting poles, you can introduce a small schooling fence some 2.7 m (9 ft) away from the last pole.

TYPES OF FENCE

There are four types of fence; they are described according to their shape. Different shapes present different degrees of difficulty.

The easiest type is the *sloping or ascending fence*, of which the triple bar is the best example. The lowest element consists of a pole at or near ground level at the front of the fence. The rest of the fence ascends away from the direction of approach. The next fence in the difficulty rating is the *pyramid* (tiger trap or double oxer), in which the middle section is the highest part. Then comes the *upright* (post and rails, gate), sometimes called a *vertical*. To judge the take-off point correctly for this type of fence, remember that the distance between the take-off point and the base of the fence should be about equal to the height of the fence. The most difficult fence to jump is the *true parallel* (parallel bars or planks with a pole behind). Both parts of the parallel should be of the same height.

BUILDING JUMPS

Ready-made show-jumps are expensive to buy. Young riders have been known to mortgage their birthday and Christmas presents for years to come in exchange for a set of six professionally built fences, but not everyone has even that opportunity. Most people make do with what they can find around home, and there is no end to the ingenuity that goes into the making of a home-made jumping course.

If there is any money available for jumps, it is best to spend it on proper poles. Jumping stands and wings can be devised and built out of a variety of materials, but poles need to be fairly heavy and substantial to be safe to use.

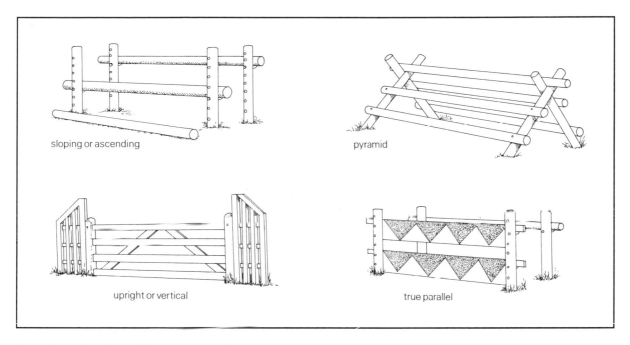

sloping or ascending

pyramid

upright or vertical

true parallel

Examples of the four different types of fence.

They should, for example, be not less than 10 cm (4 in) in diameter and at least 3 m (10 ft) long, and even unpainted poles of this description are expensive to buy.

To be able to build a reasonable jumping course, you will need at least four jumps, of which one or two should be spreads. This adds up to at least six pairs of jump stands and a few fillers to supplement the poles.

Making your own jumps

If you are good with your hands and can do some carpentry – or know someone who can – it is worth buying wood from a timber yard and making jump stands that match the professional ones. You will need metal cups to fit your home-made stands, but your jumps will look good and should last. If you are hopeless at carpentry, there is no need to despair; many other things can be used to make jumps.

Oil drums Large oil drums can be used in two ways. Standing on end, with blocks fitted to them to support poles, they make sturdy jump stands. Laid on their sides, they make a substantial filler. If you use them on their sides, bang wooden pegs into the ground on each side so that the drums cannot roll. You can paint the drums bright colours.

To make the most of a small number of oil drums, cut them in half and fix each half to an upright post to create stable jump stands. The advantage of using only half an oil drum is that the stands are reasonably light to move about.

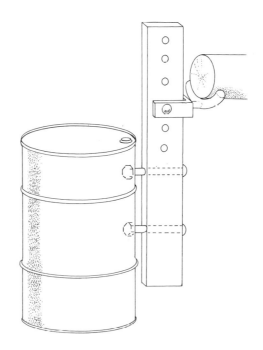

A large oil drum used as jump stand.

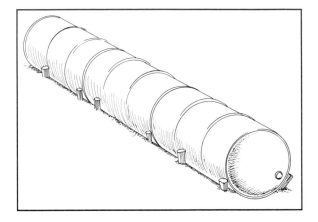

Oil drums laid on their sides and pegged to prevent them from rolling, make an inviting fence.

Old oil drums can often be obtained from factories which have no further use for them once the contents are finished. If you approach the manager or foreman, you may be able to buy the drums very cheaply. Try to get ones which are not rusty, and paint them with a metal primer as soon as you get them home. Always use a non-toxic paint, especially if the jumps are to stay in the same field as your pony, just in case he takes it into his head to lick the paint.

Plastic chemical containers These containers come in various sizes, having been used to hold fertilizers or swimming-pool chemicals.

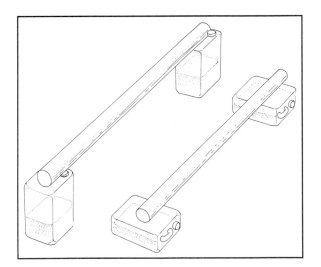

Plastic containers filled with water provide a stable base for a jump. They can be used either upright or on their sides, to vary the height of the poles.

Farmers or owners of large swimming-pools may be willing to sell them to you at a low price. Like the drums, they can be painted in bright colours, but you should always rinse them thoroughly before use. If you half-fill them with water, they will stand upright.

The containers can be used to support poles at different heights, depending on whether they are on their sides or not. A row of them makes a good filler.

Wooden pallets

Many industrial sites and factories have old pallets which they no longer need. A polite word with the foreman will often allow you to pick over the ones they have discarded and intend to burn, and you will be able to take away as many as you need. You can cut them in half horizontally and use them as a framework for a brush filler, stuffing the middle with brushwood and trimming the tops.

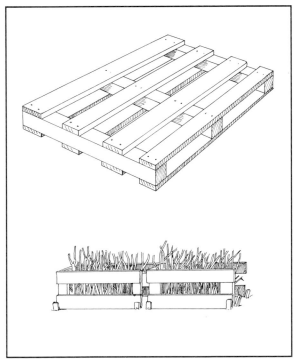

An old pallet, cut in half and filled with brushwood, can be turned into an effective brush fence.

Alternatively, face them with plywood or hardboard and paint them to resemble a wall. It may be necessary to fit supports to the bases to make them stand upright.

Pole-cups

These are expensive to buy, and you will need a large number if you are to give your

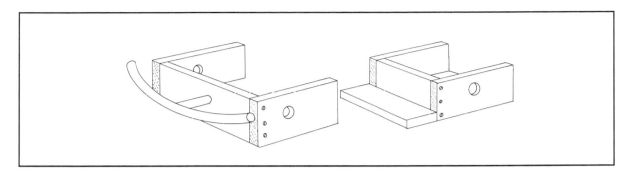

Home-made pole-cups, using wood offcuts or pieces of metal.

jumping course plenty of variety. You can, however, make quite adequate pole-cups out of wooden off-cuts (obtainable cheaply at most timber yards).

Old tyres

An inviting schooling fence can be made with old tyres, matched as far as possible for size and thickness. Thread them on to a pole and hang the pole on two stands so that the bottom of the tyres is just resting on the ground. Tyre replacement centres may let you have a number of tyres for nothing if you explain why you want them.

A jump made from old tyres threaded on to a pole.

Construction of a jumping course

The simplest layout for a jumping course is a figure of eight. Some jumps can be taken from either direction, but you should never try to jump a fence that slopes towards you because the pony can easily get too close at take-off.

All fences should have a good, easily visible ground line because a pony judges his point of take-off from the lowest part of the fence.

Always remove spare pole-cups from jump stands. If a pony jumps crookedly, he could catch a leg on a projecting cup.

Fences should look solid, rather than airy. Fillers, even if only a row of oilcans, are used for this reason. When you raise the height of a post and rail fence, always add an extra pole

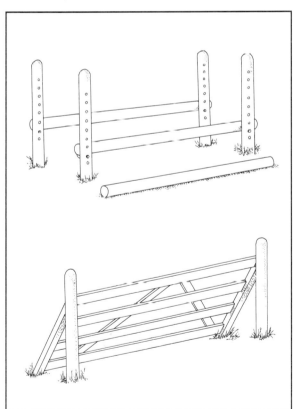

Ground lines are necessary to enable the pony to judge his point of take-off. **Top** A true ground line. **Bottom** A false ground line. It is dangerous to attempt a jump that slopes towards you as the pony cannot judge his take-off correctly and will probably get too close.

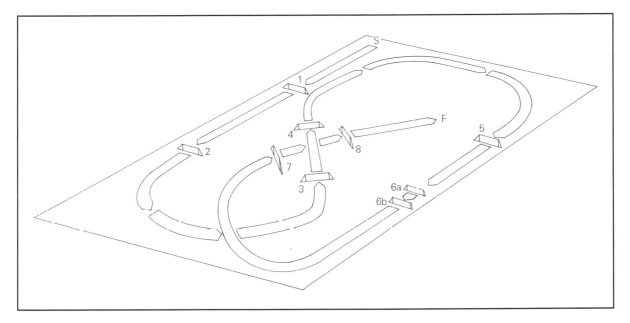

A simple figure-of-eight jumping course, using eight fences.

Number of non-jumping strides	PONY		HORSE	
	Trot	Canter	Trot	Canter
Two	9.1 m (30 ft)	9.4 10.3 m (31 34 ft)	9.1 9.7 m (30 32 ft)	10.3–10.9 m (34–36 ft)
One	4.8–5.4 m (16–18 ft)	6.4–7.3 m (21–24 ft)	5.4 m (18 ft)	7.3–8.0 m (24–26½ ft)
None (Bounce)	2.7–3.0 m (9–10 ft)	3.0–3.6 m (10–12 ft)	2.7–3.3 m (9 11 ft)	3.3 4.2 m (11 14 ft)

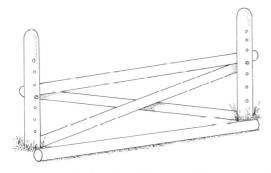

When raising the height of a fence, add two crossed poles to fill in the gap under the top pole, so that the jump is not too airy.

or use crossed poles under the top pole, to give a more solid appearance.

Never use a plank on the further side of a parallel fence.

Combinations are easier to take if the first element is an ascending jump. When building a double, it is important that the two elements are the correct distance apart; the table above gives an approximate guide. The distance varies according to the number of strides you decide to have between the two elements and the pace at which the fence will be approached. If the fence is to be approached at the trot, the distance is shorter than if it is to be approached at the canter.

When building a double for a novice pony, make certain that there are two non-jumping strides between the two elements. Doubles with one non-jumping stride and 'bounce' fences (that is, with no non-jumping stride) should not be used until a pony is experienced at jumping.

Exercises done while the pony is going out at the walk, such as bending down to touch the toes, will improve the rider's balance and suppleness.

CHAPTER 14
Shows and competitive events

PREPARATION

At any show, your pony should look as smart as possible – and so should you. If you arrive at a show with the pair of you scruffy and ungroomed, you will soon get a reputation as someone who does not look after her pony properly, even if this is not true. If you cannot be bothered to remove dirt and sweat marks from your pony or to brush the tangles out of his mane and tail, he will feel uncomfortable and will certainly not give of his best. You might catch the judge's eye, but not in a complimentary way.

Preparation for shows can be divided into two types: that which is carried out at the beginning of the season, such as mane-pulling, clipping and trimming; and that which is done early on the day itself or on the evening before.

Mane- and tail-pulling
The purpose of pulling hairs from the mane and tail is to give them a tidy appearance.

The mane In the case of the mane, pulling will encourage an untidy mane to lie flat, it will reduce a very long mane to a neater length, and will thin out an over-thick mane, making it easier to plait. You should always start with the underside of the mane, removing a few long hairs at a time, by wrapping them around your fingers or around a mane comb and pulling them out quickly with a swift tug. Always do this when the pony is warm, such as just after exercise, as the pores of the skin will be open and the hairs will come out more easily. Never pull hairs from the top of the mane, and take care not to end up with several short hairs which will stick up when the mane is plaited.

The tail The tail is pulled around the dock area and makes the top of the tail look neat and tidy. It saves the bother of plaiting it for showing classes. The tail on a pony kept at grass, however, should *never* be pulled, as he

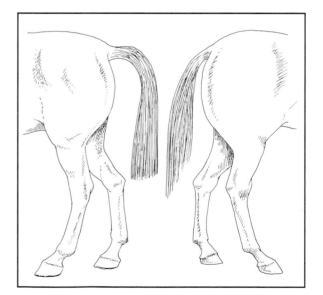

Left A bang tail, unpulled. **Right** A switch tail.

needs the bushy hairs around the top of the tail for protection against the weather.

To pull a tail, first brush it thoroughly to remove any tangles. Then dampen the top of the tail with a water brush. Pull hairs from the underneath part first, then gradually work downwards and sideways, removing hair evenly from both sides of the tail. Stop pulling when you reach a point about half-way down the tail bone.

To finish off, ask someone to hold the tail in a natural position by putting her arm under the root of the tail and lifting it. Using scissors, cut off the ends square at a point just below the hocks. This is known as a *bang tail*. Alternatively, you can continue pulling the tail much further down, leaving the ends of the tail hairs growing to a natural point. This is a *switch tail*.

When pulling is finished, use a tail bandage to preserve the shape (see page 62).

Tail-pulling is the only occasion when a mane comb can be used on the tail, and then only to help with the pulling. A mane comb used on the tail can break or split the hairs. Clippers and scissors should never be used on either a mane or tail, except to trim the end of the tail (using scissors), or to cut short a small section of mane in front of the withers, and on the poll where the headpiece of the bridle rests.

Other trimming
Scissors or clippers may be used in summer to tidy up the fetlock regions and to remove unnecessary feather. In winter, however, a grass-kept pony must be allowed to keep his fetlocks well feathered as the hair there helps to protect his heels. Overlong whiskers around the muzzle may also be trimmed in summer.

Clipping
Clipping is the removal of all or part of the pony's coat in order to stop him from sweating too much during heavy work; to enable him to do the work without getting too hot and to dry off quickly afterwards; and to make grooming easier.

Full clip All the coat is removed, including the head and legs. It should only be used on a pony which lives in throughout the winter.

A hunter clip.

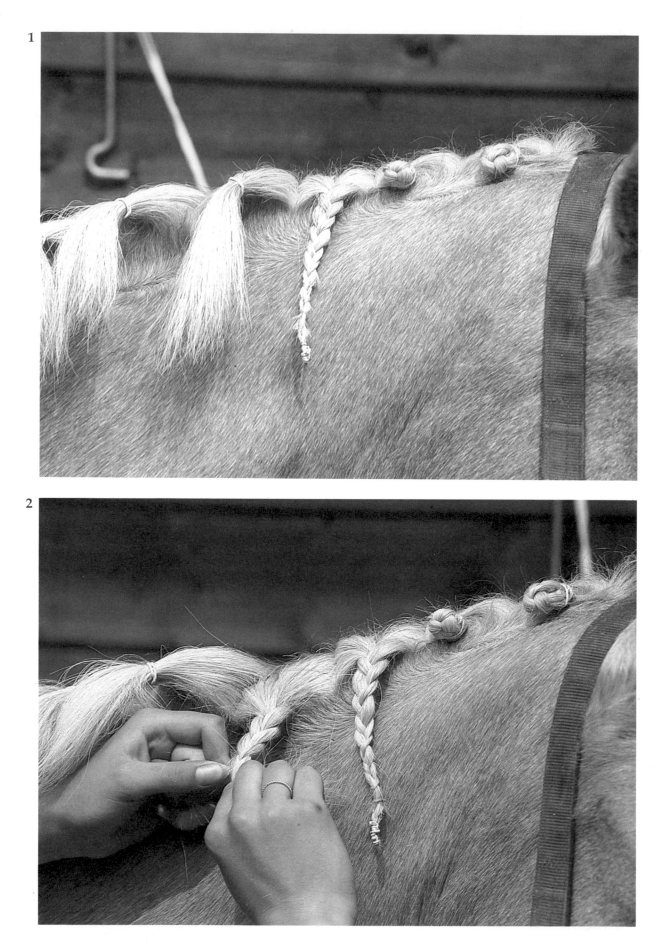

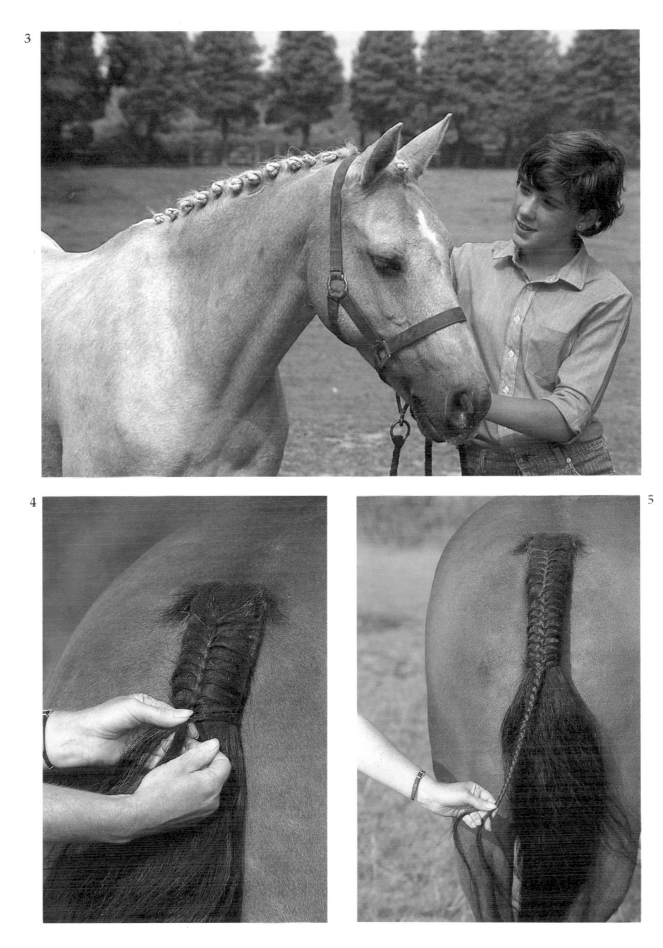

Top Blanket clip **Above** Trace high clip.
Pages 132–3 Getting ready for a show. Mane plaiting. **1** Always start at the head-end and divide the hair into the appropriate number of plaits with rubber bands. **2** Try to make the plaits the same size and evenly spaced. **3** The finished plaits make the pony look smart and help to show off his neck and head. Tail-plaiting. **4** The plait should lie centrally down the tail and the hairs drawn in from either side should be regular in size and spacing. **5** Finish off by making one long plait down the full length of the tail before bending it up to form a loop.

The belly clip, is a useful clip for a pony wintering out.

Hunter clip All the coat is removed except for a patch on the back in the shape of a saddle and on the legs as far up as the elbows and thighs. The reason for leaving some of the coat on is to give the pony protection from cold, mud, thorns and cracked heels while hunting, and to prevent the saddle from causing a sore back. A pony with this sort of clip can be turned out into a field during the day in winter, provided he is given a well-fitting New Zealand rug, but he must be brought into a stable at night.

Blanket clip An area of the coat in the shape of a blanket is left on the body and on the legs. It is often used on ponies which are stabled at night but live in a field during the day. The pony will need a New Zealand rug when he is in the field.

Trace-high clip The hair is removed only from the belly and underside of the neck, and on the outside of the flanks and front legs in a position corresponding to where the traces would go on a harness horse. It is a popular clip for ponies kept permanently at grass. Ponies with this clip would usually wear a New Zealand rug.

Belly clip This is an excellent clip for ponies living out all the time. The coat is re-moved under the belly, between the forelegs and in a narrow strip up the lower part of the neck. A pony with this clip will not get too hot while out hunting or on a strenuous ride. He would not need a New Zealand rug since the rug would not cover the clipped areas anyway.

If you want to have your pony clipped, you should ask an experienced person to do it. Clipping requires some skill as the machine head must not be allowed to overheat (most people nowadays use electric clippers). The machine needs to be well oiled, so that it is not too noisy, and the blades should be sharp. Obviously, there has to be a first time for everyone, but if you wish to do your own clipping, you should carry it out under super-vision, however calm your pony may be.

Turn-out for competitions

In some competitions a plaited mane is obligatory. In any showing class, except in-hand and ridden classes for registered native ponies, where a flowing mane and tail are characteristics of the breed, you would be ex-pected to present your pony with the mane and tail plaited up. The original reason for plaiting was to display the pony's neckline to

the best advantage, and it has now become part of turn-out requirements. Showing classes include working hunter pony events, where, although the showing is secondary to the jumping, display and turn-out are still important. You should plait for any dressage competition, including the dressage phase of a one-day event. You should also plait when going hunting. You need not plait, however, for show-jumping and cross-country, although many people do.

Plaiting

The mane A really neat row of plaits, of matching size and evenly spaced, can be achieved only by practice, so never be depressed at your first efforts. You can only improve. It does not matter how many plaits you have as long as there is an odd number along the neck, plus one for the forelock. For the best results, do not shampoo your pony's mane just before you intend to plait. Like human hair, a clean, shampooed mane becomes slippery and fly-away and is almost impossible to plait neatly. It is easier to make tight little plaits if the hair of the mane is slightly greasy.

The quick and easy way is to use rubber bands on each plait. Dampen the mane with a water brush, and divide it into the number of plaits you intend to do. Plait each section in turn, winding a rubber band several times round the end of each plait. Your pony now has a row of little pigtails along his neck. Each pigtail must now be rolled up into a tight ball and secured with another band. The plaits should always be rolled under and fit snugly against the crest.

When rubber bands are used alone, the plaits are easier to undo at the end of the day. They can work loose and one or two may come undone completely, but this method is by far the quickest if you are in a hurry.

For more secure and, on the whole, neater plaits, sewing is the best method. Even when sewing, many people use rubber bands to secure the ends of the pigtails, turning to needle and thread to keep the plaits tight when they are rolled up. You will need a reel of button thread in a colour that matches your pony's mane, and a needle with a large eye. After completing the pigtails, cut off a length of thread and pass it through the needle. Take a few turns of the thread round the end of the plait, fold it under once and push the needle through the plait about half-way up. Fold the plait under once more and push the needle through again. Wind the thread tightly round the plait, secure the ends and cut off the thread close to the plait.

Plaiting is best done on the morning of the show, but it is a lengthy business and if you are worried about time you can plait the night before. Never, however, plait the night before if your pony is in the field overnight. He will almost certainly rub the plaits which could damage the mane or, at best, you will have to do them all over again in the morning.

With a stabled pony, some people plait to the pigtail stage the previous evening and tackle the sewing stage in the morning. Alternatively, a good way of preserving the plaits overnight is to cover the whole row of plaits with an old nylon stocking, using a rubber band to hold it in place over each plait.

The tail Tail plaiting is an excellent way of making the top of the tail look neat without depriving a grass-kept pony of the protection a full tail provides. To plait the tail, start at the top, taking in a few hairs from either side in turn, until the plait reaches about two-thirds of the length of the dock. Continue plaiting downwards, using only the centre hairs, until you have a long pigtail hanging the full length of the tail. Secure the end tightly with thread. Fold the end under to form a loop and stitch it to the plait at the point where you stopped taking in side hairs.

Pages 136–7 Correct wear for pony and rider for different types of competition. Page 136: **Top** For show-jumping tweed hacking jackets are usually worn. **Bottom left** A plain coloured jacket for a showing class. **Bottom right** A tweed jacket for Pony Club dressage. This photograph was taken before the present Pony Club regulations regarding hats came into force. Nowadays, the rider would be wearing a hat that conforms to the regulations set out on page 59. Page 137: For cross-country riding, protection is needed for both pony and rider. A young rider models two forms of protective wear. **Top left and right** the jockey skull cap, fitted with a chin strap and over which a plain or coloured silk is worn, and the back protector, which goes under the jersey or jacket. Instead of a back protector, the rider could wear a body protector, which is shaped like a tunic. Both back and body protectors guard the spine and ribs from injury. **Bottom** A surcingle should be put on over the saddle as a safeguard against accidents should the girth break. The reins are rubber-covered to prevent the rider's hands from slipping. The pony has all four legs bandaged against raps and tendon injury.

Always undo all plaiting as soon as you have finished the classes in which plaits are needed. Use small, sharp, pointed scissors – embroidery scissors are best – and snip the threads carefully, making certain that you do not cut the hair at the same time.

TYPES OF SHOW

Show-jumping

Most local shows hold show-jumping competitions, usually restricted to competitors of a certain age or ponies of a certain height. Novice competitions are generally open to combinations (that is, pony and rider together) who have not won a jumping event. Other novice classes are described as £10 Novice or £30 Novice. This means that the total winnings of the combination must not exceed that amount. So, even if you have had some success already, you may still be eligible for a novice event. All these classes are described as *unaffiliated* and, although they are usually judged by the rules of the British Show Jumping Association (BSJA), there may be local variations. Prize money cannot exceed an amount stipulated by the BSJA.

Affiliated classes are quite a different matter. To be eligible to compete in affiliated shows, you must be a paid up member of the British Show Jumping Association and your pony must be registered with the BSJA. Novice ponies are registered JC (Junior Grade C) but will be upgraded to JA (Junior Grade A) when their winnings reach a certain figure. The jumps in these classes will be of a stipulated height, and the speed at which the course should be jumped is also laid down. If you are not a member of the BSJA, even if you buy a registered jumping pony, you cannot compete in affiliated shows.

In the USA some shows are affiliated with the American Horse Shows Association (AHSA); others that are not are called 'non-recognized' shows. Novice classes in the USA are referred to as 'green' or 'maiden' events. Novice ponies competing in AHSA recognized shows are also classified by their earnings.

The Preliminary horse will be upgraded to an Intermediate horse, once his earnings have reached a certain level.

Working hunter pony

Classes for working hunter ponies (WHP) have become very popular in recent years. They were started in response to a demand for some type of showing class for ponies which would carry their young riders safely out hunting and were nice-looking ponies although not quite good enough for purely showing events.

Competitors in these classes start off by jumping a course of natural fences – not coloured ones – and those which have not been eliminated in the jumping phase are then judged on conformation. Although, as in any showing class, the result depends on the opinion of the judges, a nice, forward-going pony which jumps the course confidently and willingly should have the edge on a pony which may be beautiful to look at but is an unwilling or hesitant jumper. There are usually five separate WHP classes: Cradle Stakes, for ponies 12 hh and under, ridden by children aged nine years and under; Nursery Stakes, for ponies exceeding 12 hh but not exceeding 13 hh, ridden by children aged eleven years and under; 13 hh and under, riders fourteen years and under; over 13 hh but not exceeding 14 hh, riders sixteen and under; over 14 hh but not exceeding 15 hh, riders eighteen and under.

A recently-introduced show category is the class for ponies of hunter type. The ponies are similar to WHP entries but are not asked to complete a jumping course.

Hunter trials

These are cross-country events, in which riders have to complete a course of fixed fences at a fair hunting pace. There is often a timed section, with a gate to be opened and closed. The winner is not necessarily the fastest, as most hunter trials have what is known as a bogey time, which is not revealed to the competitors but which is worked out by

Pages 140–41 A typical cross-country fence, well ridden. **Top left** The horse approaches the fence, the rider having previously walked the course and settled on the best line. **Bottom left** As the horse lands, the rider is already looking towards the next fence. **Right** A clean, neat turn. The rider's weight is well forward to free the pony's loins and encourage speed.

the organizers according to the length of the course. Time penalties are given to those riders who exceed or fall short of the time allowed, and are added to any penalties gathered during the round. Penalties are given for refusals (three refusals at any one jump usually means elimination) and for falls while tackling a jump. A fall in between fences is not penalized. In pairs events, where two competitors ride round the course together, there are generally two or three dressing fences which the riders must take abreast, and they will earn penalties if they are not together. At some hunter trials, marks for style are also given. Competitors in hunter trials are expected to wear tweed jackets, although they may wear crash helmets with dark blue or black silk hat covers.

Competitors wear bibs with their number printed on, so that the number can be seen clearly by the fence judges. You will usually be asked for a small deposit when you collect your numbered bib, which you get back when you return your number. You should always check, when you collect your number, whether you will be riding in numerical order or whether you have to declare at the start. If the latter, this means that you give your number to the starter's steward who will enter it on a list on a blackboard. Always allow yourself plenty of time to warm up before the start.

One-day events

The one-day event consists of three disciplines: dressage, cross-country and show-jumping. Usually the show-jumping phase follows the cross-country, but this depends on the organizers. The dressage phase is always first.

The dressage phase The dressage test to be used will be given on the schedule, and a copy of the test can usually be obtained from the organizers. When you make your entry, you may be asked to enclose a stamped addressed envelope so that your dressage time may be sent to you, or you may have to telephone the organizers a day or two before the event. The time given to you may seem rather odd: 11.14 a.m., for example, or 12.08 p.m. The reason for this precision is that organizers allow seven minutes per competitor (five minutes for the test and two minutes for the judge to write up any comments).

Dress for the dressage test is: jacket, tie,

velvet-covered hard hat. In Pony Club competitions, this hat must conform to BS4472, although it does not have to be a skull-cap with cover (see page 59). Present yourself to the dressage steward at least ten minutes before your test is due and spend the intervening period walking your pony round quietly. When the competitor before you leaves the dressage arena, the steward will indicate that it is now your turn. This does not mean that you immediately rush into the arena but simply that you should start walking your pony quietly round the perimeter of the arena on the outside, thus showing to the judge that you are ready to begin when invited to. The signal to start may be a bell or a car horn. When you hear it, you continue round the arena until you reach the entrance at the marker 'A'.

In Pony Club dressage tests – and these include one-day events – certain rules are laid down. You cannot, for example, ride your pony in a double bridle; a snaffle should be worn, although a drop noseband or martingale is acceptable. The rider may carry a whip but is not allowed to wear spurs. The pony may not be shown in leg bandages, brushing boots or overreach boots. You must wear a crash helmet.

In dressage, each part of the test is marked out of ten, and the marks gained are totalled and taken away from the maximum score. The figure obtained is your dressage score and the lower it is, the better.

The cross-country phase In some one-day events, you will be given a starting time for the cross-country phase, and for the show-jumping. There will always be plenty of time for you to change out of your dressage clothes and into your cross-country clothing. Most people like to ride in colours, a striped rugby shirt or jersey, with complementary coloured silk for the crash helmet. Wear the best protective clothing available: a proper crash helmet (BS4472) with harness, and some form of body protection.

The *back* protector is made of expanded polystyrene which may be reinforced down the centre. It is usually curved to guard against rib injuries, is held in position by a strap round the waist and is worn under the shirt or jersey.

The *body* protector is also worn under clothing and many riders find it more comfortable. It is shaped like a waistcoat or tunic and is fitted with pockets back and front which contain pieces of polystyrene. It extends protection to the front of the body as well as the back and, because the shock-absorbing material is in sections, gives the wearer greater freedom of movement.

Neither type of protector has yet become compulsory wear for Pony Club members (although point-to-point riders do have to wear one), but will no doubt become so once a satisfactory standard has been established.

The pony should also wear some sort of protective clothing, such as overreach boots and or leg bandages. A cross-country surcingle which passes over the saddle and round the pony's girth is a useful safety measure against the saddle girths suddenly breaking. The sur-cingle has an elasticated inset to stop it from restricting the pony's movements.

The show-jumping phase The rider should change back into jacket and tie. Formal dress should always be worn for the prize-giving, if you are lucky or skilful enough to get into the rosettes.

Combined training
This competition consists of two phases: dressage and show-jumping. The dressage phase always takes place first.

Part III
First Horse

CHAPTER 15
Choosing the right horse

Choice of horse is, perhaps, even more important than choice of pony. The capital cost of a horse is likely to be three, four or even five times that of a pony, and when you are spending thousands rather than hundreds, mistakes are expensive. But there is a more subtle reason. Someone switching from ponies to horses is usually acknowledging that he or she intends to carry on riding, that what has been a pleasant pastime is now worthy of a more serious approach, and that they may even make a career with or relating to horses.

One of the first things you have to decide is whether you are looking for a 'made' horse or for one which you can train yourself. It depends on your attitude. A highly-competitive rider may prefer to take over a horse which has already proved itself in the show-ring. Another may prefer training a horse to competing, but this calls for a patient temperament and plenty of spare time.

Made horses will clearly cost more to buy than a young horse or a green one. To buy an unschooled horse with potential is more of a gamble, but provided that your judgement is sound it is more satisfying than following in someone else's successful footsteps.

So be honest with yourself. Examine your motives carefully and look ahead as far as you can. Is this a short-term project? If you are approaching the gap between school and college, are you looking for one short successful season? Will you, in a year or eighteen months' time, still have the energy, desire and hours available to continue your horse's schooling programme? Bear in mind that what was true for ponies–namely that it can take six months, a year or even longer for rider and pony to build up a really good relationship–is just as true for horses.

One of the most important facts to remember is that a horse is not just a large pony. Most ponies, even those of indeterminate breed, have sufficient native blood in their veins to respond happily to little work or lots. They are fairly easy to keep since most of them will live out, and need a less arduous routine to make them fit enough to take part in competiton.

Horses, most of whom have some Thoroughbred in their ancestry, are much greedier of your time and attention. They certainly cannot winter out, even though they may live out during the summer months. Because they are physically bigger, everything connected with them is more expensive. Shoeing bills, for example, are likely to be higher and to occur more often. They eat more food, their worming dosages are higher, and items of tack and clothing are dearer.

If you settled for a small stable when you had a pony, you will now be faced with finding or building a bigger loose box. If you have a small pony trailer, you now need one capable of carrying a horse in safety and comfort. A bigger trailer, with a heavier occupant, may require a bigger car.

Examine all the pros and cons carefully, find out as much as you can from friends with horses, talk it over with your parents–and then decide. The ways of finding a horse are no different from finding a pony. Word-of-mouth, advertisements, or a dealer are the principal sources of horses for sale. It is mainly the purchase price that changes.

WHAT TYPE OF HORSE?

Many riders aged seventeen plus, who, as associate members of the Pony Club, are still eligible to take part in Pony Club activities and compete in Pony Club competitions and team events, are looking for a horse which is capable of taking them over the bigger courses found in competitions at this level. By this age, they have usually decided on the type of riding they most enjoy and are often prepared to work harder than younger children to achieve their goal.

In an event like the tetrathlon, for example, which comprises the four disciplines: shooting, swimming, riding and running, a great deal of effort will be put into improving performance in the shooting, swimming and running phases. But if the pony cannot tackle the cross-country course, which although not difficult does have obstacles up to a height of 1.07 m (3 ft 6 in), much of that effort will have been wasted. So a young tetrathlon enthusiast will be looking for a horse on which she can approach the cross-country phase with confidence.

Fences in show jumping and eventing competitions are also higher at Pony Club associate level, while the keen dressage competitor may be anxious to progress to the more advanced tests.

There is often, too, a desire to improve for improvement's sake and to feel that progress is not only possible but being achieved.

For the really keen young rider, there is enormous satisfaction to be gained in taking an untrained horse and building up his confidence and experience gradually until, some eighteen months or two years later, he can be truly described as a polished performer. Or, if you want to look even further ahead, you might wish to start with an unbroken youngster and bring him to the peak of his potential entirely yourself.

BREEDS OF HORSE

The riding horse is not as easy to define, in terms of breeding, as the mountain or moorland pony. For example, with the nine breeds of pony indigenous to the British Isles very clear rules are laid down by the breed societies and cover such characteristics as height, colour, markings and shape. A horse, however, is roughly defined as standing more than 14.2 hh at the withers; and a riding horse is one which is a comfortable ride.

Many of today's riding horses have an ancestry in which such varied types as Thoroughbred, Arab, carriage horse, draught horse and native pony are combined. The Hunters' Improvement Society has, in the hundred years since it was formed, made great efforts to establish a good hunter type, principally by its Premium Schemes for stallions and mares and by organizing important shows.

The qualities required by a good hunter are a calm temperament, boldness, strength and stamina. These will stand it in good stead in the hunting field, where it may be called upon to stand around for long periods, gallop for long stretches, tackle big or tricky fences in muddy or hard going, in and out of woods, and possibly to keep going for several hours. These qualities are also of value in the show-jumping arena and the eventing field.

The hunter should have a deep, wide chest, with plenty of heart room, short back and sloping shoulder, strong muscular loins and quarters. Its legs must be clean and strong, with good bone, knees large, hocks large and bony. Its hooves should be big and open, with hard horn and a well-developed frog. The head must be lean, small-muzzled and well-boned, with a bold but kindly eye.

The deeper the girth and the bigger the bone (that is, the circumference of the leg measured just below the knee), the greater the weight the horse is able to carry.

Some of the best hunters have been half-breeds; by a Thoroughbred stallion out of a draught mare, the first for speed and quality, the second for strength. Cross-breeding, however, has produced a variety of types, and in recent years many of the Continental breeds have become popular for dressage, show-jumping and eventing. Of these, the German Hanoverian is one of the most liked, possibly because it seems to have an inbred love of competition and showmanship, although it was originally bred as a carriage horse.

Page 148 Riding out for relaxation. A rider usually makes the change from pony to horse because he or she intends to take a more serious approach to what was previously a hobby – probably by moving on to a higher level of competition. However, it is important to continue to enjoy the pleasures of riding as well.

In fact, it is the carriage horses of the past which are much in demand today for all forms of competition: the English Cleveland Bay, the German Oldenburg and Trakehner, the Dutch Gelderland, the Swiss Einsiedler, and many others. Ireland, where the Irish or English Thoroughbred was first crossed with a draught mare to produce a fine hunter, still breeds some of the best horses in the world.

The Arab horse has fanatical support throughout the world. Pure-bred Arab studs can be found in many countries, and the Arab-Thoroughbred cross, known as the Anglo-Arab, combines the qualities of both, particularly the beauty and presence of the Arab with the extra height and speed of the Thoroughbred.

In the USA, many of the individual saddle-horse breeds have been developed with a particular purpose in mind. The Quarter Horse, for example, capable of the short bursts of speed and extreme agility which are necessary in controlling cattle, is an unrivalled cow-pony. Some of the saddle horses from the southern states, the Tennessee Walking Horse or Kentucky Saddler, have additional gaits which are very comfortable and showy. Others are bred for their markings: the Appaloosa or the Pinto, for example.

Most of the horses used for show-jumping and eventing in the USA are descended from horses imported from Europe during the twentieth century, mostly from the British Isles, but increasingly from Germany as well.

Page 149 A horse and rider going well in a cross-country event. A great deal of time and dedication is needed to look after a horse that is going to be ridden in competitions such as two- and three-day events.

CHAPTER 16
Stabling

There is only one way to get a horse really fit and that is to keep him stabled. When a horse is indoors day and night, you have precise control over his feeding and exercise programmes and can chart his progress exactly.

Fitness is all important in a horse competing at an advanced level. When you are entering two- and three- day events with their additional roads and tracks and steeplechase phases, your horse needs to be as well tuned as you can make him, with not an ounce of surplus fat on him and his muscles well developed. If your interest is hunting, and you can afford both the time and money to hunt two or three days a week, your horse must be able to cope with the demands you make on him.

It is very important, therefore, to see that his living conditions are the best you can provide.

SUITABLE LOOSE BOX

A large loose box allows a horse some freedom of movement, and this is needed to prevent physical problems developing, such as filled legs caused by standing in one place for too long; and problems of behaviour, such as weaving or crib-biting, which are caused by boredom. The loose box, therefore, should be at least 3.6 × 3.3 m (12 × 11 ft) and nearer to 3.6 × 4.3 m (12 × 14 ft) if possible. A large box will also encourage the horse to lie down and rest from time to time, and this is important to his well being.

Doors
The doorway must be wide enough to allow a horse to pass through it in comfort: at least

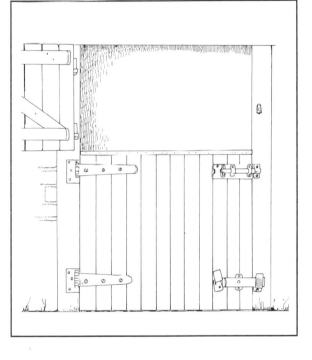

The stable door should be wide enough to allow a horse to pass in and out without banging himself.

1.25 m (4 ft) wide. The door itself should be in two halves, so that the top half can be fastened back, and the animal can look out over the bottom half to watch what is going on. Horses are herd animals by instinct, and need the company of other living creatures. Failing other horses, just the comings and goings of human beings will help to keep them mentally content. A single stable should, if possible, be sited in a place where there is plenty of activity during the day.

Horses can feel claustrophobic, just as humans do, so always give your horse as large a stable as possible. Keep the fittings to a minimum to reduce risk of injury.

Floor

Many years ago, stable floors were made of wood, usually blocks of hard wood. The only advantage of this type of flooring was that it was warm. Wood, however, is absorbent and in a stable in constant use, it is almost permanently damp so that it is neither very durable nor very hygienic.

Wooden floors were succeeded in due course by brick ones; very hard, blue bricks with grooved surfaces were usually used. These can still be seen in old stables attached to old houses and, provided they are still in reasonably good condition, there is no need to replace them with a concrete floor.

Nowadays, most stables, especially the prefabricated timber stables which are widely available, are erected on a concrete floor. Concrete is hard-wearing, and if the surface is roughened slightly it need not be slippery. To help the drainage, the floor should slope a little towards a shallow drainage channel at the front of the box. The slope should not be more than one in sixty; a greater gradient can be tiring for the horse.

Roof

A double-pitched roof is the most attractive, but a single pitch is cheaper. The internal height should not be less than 3 m (10 ft) high, except where roof and walls meet, when 2.7 m (9 ft) is sufficient. This height is necessary in order that a horse does not injure himself if he throws up his head. A sloping roof should run from front to back. Whatever type of roof the stable has, it must be well insulated. An overhang at the front of the box will give some protection against rain and sunshine.

Ventilation

Fresh air is vital, but draughts should be prevented. Most prefabricated stables have a window, which should be protected by a grille. The top half of a stable window is often hinged along its bottom edge so that it opens inwards and the air is directed above the

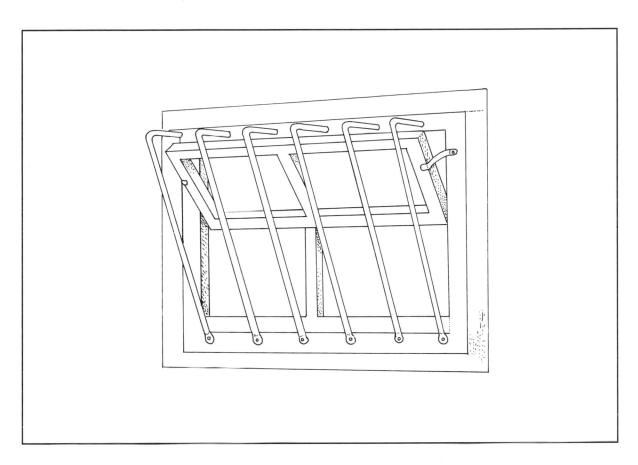

Windows should be protected by bars. If they open, it is best that they open inwards at the top, so that the incoming air is directed over the horse's head.

horse's head. However, as long as the loose box is protected from the prevailing wind – by other buildings or a high hedge or fence – the open top half of the door (securely fastened back) will provide adequate ventilation. If you are worried that your horse might jump out, the opening can be fitted with a mesh grille or even removable bars.

Lighting

When a horse is kept permanently in a stable, much of the work inside the box in winter will be done after dark, so good lighting is needed. Wall lights are best as they throw light into all corners of the box and cast the fewest shadows, but they should be bulkhead fittings, or covered by a metal grille. A suspended bulb is better than no light at all. It should not hang lower than 3 m (10 ft) above the ground, and it tends to collect dust and cobwebs. All cables inside the box should run through galvanized metal conduits fixed out of the horse's reach, or else be cut into the wall. Switches and power points, properly insulated, must be outside the box, unless the switch is the pull-sort used in bathrooms.

Outside the loose box

A small pen or yard adjoining the stable cannot be beaten for convenience and security. The horse can be turned out there while you are cleaning out the box. It need be no more than a concrete hard standing, enclosed by a post-and-rail fence, with slip rails to shut off the entrance.

STABLE FITTINGS

The less there is in the stable, the better. Water, however, should be available at all times and this can be supplied either in buckets or to an automatic drinking trough. The latter consists of a shallow bowl which refills automatically every time the horse drinks. It is very convenient as long as it is situated well away from the haynet so that scraps of hay cannot fall into it and interfere

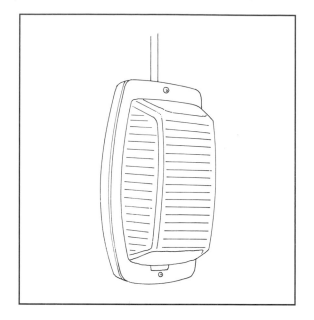

A bulkhead light fitting, fixed to the wall out of the horse's reach.

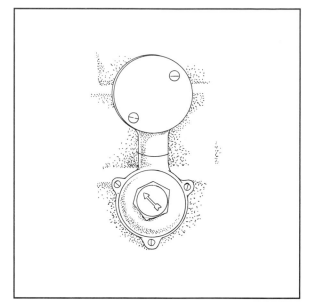

The light switch should be outside the stable and designed to protect the horse from electrocution if he should bite it.

with the mechanism. Buckets may be placed in galvanized metal bucket holders or in old car tyres to prevent them from being accidentally knocked over.

A manger is not necessary but can be useful if you are unable to visit the horse last thing at night to remove the feed bucket. If you have to feed the horse from a bucket on the floor and cannot take it away when he has finished, you are liable to find a squashed or broken bucket when you get to the stable in the morning. Many horses seem to play football with empty buckets, finally lying down on them, and quite apart from the risk of injury

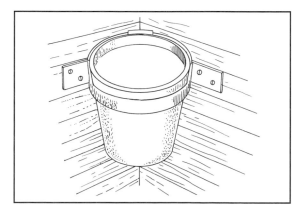

A bucket will not be kicked over if it is placed in a special bucket holder.

to the horse, no bucket in the world can stand up indefinitely to such disrespectful treatment. A removable plastic manger, set into a holder at chest height in one corner, is safe and hygienic as the bowl can be taken out for cleaning.

Tethering rings for both horse and haynets are needed. Two haynets should be available: one near the door where the horse can stand and eat while he is looking out, and the other set well away from the door and out of any draughts. The horse can be tied to the haynet rings if necessary, or you can provide separate rings at chest height for this purpose. The safest type of ring to use is the sort that is fastened to a bolt which goes right through the stable wall to a nut and washer on the outside. To tether the horse, attach a loop of haystring to the ring, and tie the horse to that. In an emergency, the string will break or can be cut. In any case, always use a quick release knot for tying up horse and haynet.

FEED STORE

A separate shed for storing foodstuffs is essential, although it can be combined with a tack-room if it is big enough. Each type of feed should have a separate container: dustbins make excellent containers as they are vermin-proof and will take a 25 kg (55 lb) sack

A cast horse is one which has rolled over too close to the wall and he cannot get sufficient purchase to enable him to roll back. If a horse does become cast, you will need assistance in getting him into a safe position. One person should sit on his neck to prevent him from struggling, while others attach ropes to his hind and forelegs. Get up from his neck and roll him over on to his other side.

If a horse has to be tethered in the stable, use the ball and rope method. This consists of a wooden ball attached to the end of the tethering rope. The rope passes through a ring and is kept taut by the weight of the ball.

The advantage of the ball and rope is that the horse has freedom to lie down without getting entangled in the rope.

of everything except bran. Bran, being a bulky food for its weight, takes up more room and two dustbins will be needed to store 25 kg (55 lb). You will also need a scoop for measuring out the food. A galvanized metal scoop can be bought from any corn chandler, or you can make one yourself from a plastic squash-bottle by cutting off the bottom at an oblique angle. The best bottles to use are the large ones with moulded handles, usually obtainable at cash-and-carry suppliers or wholesalers. Whatever scoop you use, however, weigh a heaped scoopful of each foodstuff used, so that you know exactly how much feed your horse is getting without having to resort to the scales every time.

If you have no barn or shed large enough to store hay and straw in quantity, you may have to make a stack in the open and cover it with a tarpaulin. Use wooden pallets as a base and bear in mind that, unless the tarpaulin covers the stack completely, part of every outside bale will deteriorate through exposure to the weather and you will have to throw it away. So always allow for wastage when ordering your winter supplies.

If you choose to bed your horse down on wood shavings, storage is easier when they are packed in plastic-covered bales. The plastic will protect them from the weather, but remember to check each bale to see that there are no splits or holes through which rain-water can seep.

STABLE TOOLS

Choose your stable tools carefully; look after them properly and they will last a long time. You will need a yard broom, long-handled shovel, a four-tined stable fork, a skep or muck-sack and wheelbarrow. You will also need a rake if you are using shavings or sawdust for the bedding.

Brooms The yard broom has a wooden handle and a stiff-bristled brush head, which can be replaced when it is worn out. If you buy too big a head, you will find that brushing out the stable and yard is very tiring. A smaller head is just as efficient. To prolong the life of the brush, always rinse debris and dirt off the bristles before hanging it up to dry.

Shovels A stable shovel is a broad, flat shovel with lipped sides attached to a long handle. It is best to get a light-weight aluminium shovel, which is light and easy to use.

Forks The fork has curved tines (prongs), usually four, and is used for picking up and removing droppings from the straw. It is also useful for shaking up straw when laying the bed. A pitchfork is excellent for carrying straw bales and for laying the bed, but a four-tined fork has more uses.

Skeps A skep is a rubber or wickerwork container with sloping sides and carrying handles, used for picking up and removing droppings during the day. Most people use a plastic laundry basket for this purpose as it is an excellent cheap substitute.

Sacks A muck-sack may be used instead of a skep. It is simply a square of hessian or some other material, often fitted with a handle at each corner. The droppings are tipped into the sack, the corners gathered together, and the whole bundle carried off to the muck-heap.

Wheelbarrows The wheelbarrow should be the largest you can afford, provided it is not too heavy. It is used to cart soiled straw and dung to the manure heap. Always leave it tipped up on end when not in use so that it can drain properly.

Useful extras include a two-wheeled porter's trolley for moving heavy bales of hay or straw and sacks of horse-feed. You will also need a hose-pipe for sluicing down the loose box and stable yard, for rinsing off your horse after shampooing, and for cleaning mud off his legs after hunting.

CHAPTER 17
Stable routine

It is the daily routine which really brings home the difference between owning a pony and owning a horse. Most ponies are kept at grass most of the time, although they may be stabled at night in the winter. Bringing a pony in from his field after school, turning him out the next morning and mucking out his loose box once a day, take up perhaps one hour in twenty-four. To look after a horse that is permanently stabled, including grooming and exercise, occupies a large part of the daylight hours. Unless you intend to make a career with horses, when doing your own horse may be part of your training, you will almost certainly have to fit all this in around your time at school or college, although you may be able to share the duties with a friend or a member of your family.

As horses are creatures of habit, you must work out a timetable and stick to it as closely as possible. Feeding times should not be varied at all except on special days, such as when hunting or showing. A horse seems to know his feeding time, to the minute, and if you are late he will begin to fret, stamping his feet, pawing the ground, kicking the door and the sides of his box, perhaps even picking up bad habits like crib-biting.

Draw up your timetable carefully as soon as you get your new horse. The following will remind you what has to be done. You can, of course, alter the times to suit yourself.

A DAILY TIMETABLE

7.00 a.m.   Enter the stable, put headcollar on horse and tie him up, so that you can inspect him carefully for any overnight injury.

Empty the water bucket, rinse out and refill. Offer the fresh water to the horse but do not worry if he does not want a drink.

Refill the haynet and tie it up.

Muck out the stable, removing all soiled straw and droppings. Leave the clean straw in a pile in one corner. If you use shavings, remove droppings and cut out any wet patches. Rake the bed level.

Pick out the horse's feet. If he is quiet, you can pick out each foot in turn straight into the skep, which prevents the pickings from littering the stable floor. Remove the skep or sweep up the pickings.

Quarter the horse; that is, give him a perfunctory grooming. Use a sponge to clean the eyes, nostrils and dock. Unbuckle the front of his night rug and fold it back over the surcingle or roller. Use a body brush lightly on his head, neck, chest and forelegs. Refasten the rug. Then fold back the rear of the rug and brush the horse's hindquarters. Use a water brush or sponge to get rid of any night stains. Replace the rug. Finish off by brushing out the mane and tail.

(7 a.m. cont.)

Lay the day bed by using the clean straw piled in the corner.

Prepare the horse's feed.

7.45 a.m. Give the horse his feed and leave him to eat in peace while you have your own breakfast.

9.30 a.m. Remove droppings from the stable.

Take off the night rug and tack up. Take the horse out for at least an hour's exercise. When you return, remove the saddle and bridle. Give your horse time to roll.

11 a.m. Short rack: that is, tie up the horse fairly short so that he cannot move about.

Give him a thorough groom (strapping). This should be done within twenty minutes of returning from exercise, as it is best carried out when the horse is warm and the pores of the skin are open. He should, however, be dry. If he sweats a lot during exercise you should give him time to dry off.

Strapping starts with picking out the feet. This is followed by a good going over with the dandy-brush to remove dirt and sweat. Always brush in the same direction as the lie of the coat and complete the near side before moving to the off side. Pay special attention to the saddle mark and girth area, hocks, knees, fetlocks and pasterns.

Take the body brush, push the mane to the wrong side and tackle the roots of the mane, removing all scurf and dust. Finish by bringing the mane back to the right side and brushing it carefully, working from withers to poll. Brush the forelock.

Now go over the body with the body brush, putting plenty of weight into the brushing movements. Use a circular motion, but finish in the direction of the coat, and give a slight outward flick at the end of each brush stroke to

(11 a.m. cont.)

force dirt and dust away from the body. Use a curry-comb to clean the body brush as you go.

Groom the head with the body brush. If the headcollar gets in the way, take it off and refasten it round the horse's neck.

Use the body brush on the tail, removing any tangles with the fingers.

Finish off by strapping the body thoroughly with a wisp. This action tones up the muscular parts of the body. It hardens the muscles, stimulates the oil-producing glands, improves the blood supply to the skin and brings a shine to the coat. A wisp is made from soft hay, twisted to form a rope. When the rope is about 3 m (10 ft) long, form two

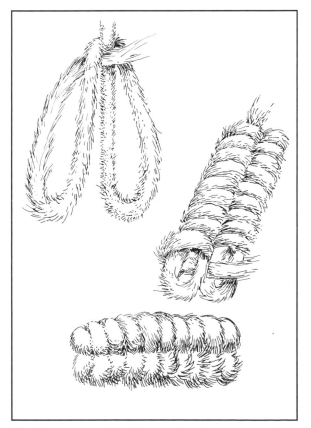

The three stages of making a wisp from a rope of a soft, twisted hay

(11 a.m. cont.)
loops at one end of it. Wind the remaining hay-rope round both loops together and finish off by passing the loose end through the loops and pulling tight. Beat the wisp on the ground, stamp on it or bang it against a wall, to flatten it. The finished wisp should not disintegrate as you use it. Effective use of the wisp requires practice and knowledge of where it will do the most good. The wisp is needed on the muscular parts of the body; the neck, the sides of the shoulders and on the quarters and thighs. Put plenty of effort into banging it hard against the horse's body, following the lie of the coat, and avoid the loins and bony parts. When you have finished the near side move round and give the off side the same treatment – and then take a short rest, because you should be feeling exhausted.

Fortunately, the next stage, by comparison, is quite restful. Using a sponge and clean water, wash around the eyelids, removing any mucus which may have collected in the corners of the eyes. Rinse the sponge out, squeeze and wipe over the lips and muzzle. Rinse once more and wipe the nostrils. Complete the washing process by sponging the dock and the underside of the tail.

Finish off the mane by using the water brush, dipped in water and shaken to remove the surplus, to smooth the hair into place.

Wash the feet (unless the weather is too cold), carefully removing any mud, and taking care not to let any water get into the hollow of the heel. If you do accidentally wet it, take care to dry it properly. If there is any sign of cracked heels or mud fever – soreness, redness of the skin (particularly noticeable on white feet)

(11 a.m. cont.)
or raw patches – dust with an antibiotic powder. Petroleum jelly, liberally smeared around the heels and over the pastern and fetlock joint, will give protection.

When the feet have dried, brush hoof oil all over the outside of the hoof wall as high as the coronet.

Use a stable rubber over the whole coat to give a last polish. Then put the day rug on the horse.

Refill the water buckets, and untie the horse. Prepare the midday feed.

12.30 p.m. Give the mid-day feed.
Refill haynet.
Tidy up the yard.

4.00 p.m. Tie up the horse and pick out his feet. Use the skep to remove droppings and shake up the bedding.
Refill water buckets.
Untie horse and prepare third feed.

4.45 p.m. Give the third feed.

7.00 p.m. Tie up the horse.
Remove droppings in skep and lay the night bed, adding enough clean, well-shaken straw to make a soft, springy bed. Make certain that the straw is well banked around the sides of the box.
Refill water buckets and haynet.
Remove day rug, and give the horse a final grooming, called setting fair. Brush him lightly all over with the body brush, and use the wisp on his muscles.
Put the night rug on him, adding a blanket underneath if the night is likely to be very cold. It is better to give the horse extra clothing to keep him warm and to leave the top half of the stable door open, than to shut the top door. Untie the horse.
Prepare the last feed.

(cont. page 162)

Pages 160–61 A bright, friendly, cheerful stable yard, which is neat and clean. Heads over the stable doors show that the horses here take an interest in everything that is going on.

7.30 p.m.   Give the final feed.

8.30 p.m.   Clean the tack, unless you have managed to fit it in during the afternoon.

10.00 p.m. Visit the stable to check that all is well. Do not go right into the stable unless the rugs have slipped and need adjusting. You should disturb the horse as little as possible.

It is obvious from the timetable that looking after a horse can be a full-time job. If you are at school or college, or are at work all day, you will certainly need a friend to help you, although there are short cuts that you can take. Grooming, for example, need not be quite so thorough, but feeding times and exercise must not be varied or skimped.

EXERCISE

Exercise for the horse can be difficult to arrange, especially in winter when it may be dark before you leave the house and after you return. You may be able to arrange to have the use of an all-weather school; fitted with floodlights if possible. An indoor school is even better, as you can then exercise at any time and in any weather. But whether it is an outdoor, floodlit manege or an indoor one, you must be able to get to it without having to do any roadwork after dark.

If there is no way in which you can exercise your horse in safety or in daylight, the only solution is to turn him out during the day. A small exercising paddock would be sufficient for him to exercise himself. Even a securely-fenced schooling arena, with a bark or wood-chip surface, is better than leaving the horse to stand all day long in a loose box. A clipped horse can be rugged up against the weather. Choose the best New Zealand rug that you can afford; if possible try to buy a self-righting one without a surcingle. Put an extra blanket underneath if the weather is very cold.

STABLE VICES

A horse that is left all day in a loose box without any form of exercise runs all sorts of risks, from filled legs to boredom. Boredom leads to stable vices, which, once established, are very difficult to cure.

The stable vice known as weaving. The horse swings his head from side to side.

One method of preventing weaving is to suspend a brick over the stable door.

Kicking the panelling

This annoying habit is disturbing to other horses, and to your neighbours if your stable is near other houses. It is dangerous, as the horse might injure himself in the process. And it is expensive if the panels have to be repaired regularly.

Weaving

The horse moves his head from side to side, often shifting his weight in a rocking movement from one foot to another. It is a common vice, and causes problems because the horse is using up energy and can lose weight as a result. Sometimes, the horse likes to have his head over the stable door while he is weaving. A grille or bars fitted over the opening may discourage him. The cause is nearly always lack of exercise and boredom. More exercise or a change of scenery could cure it altogether.

Crib-biting

The horse takes hold of the edge of the stable door or manger with his teeth, sucks in air and swallows it. It is damaging to the horse because it causes indigestion and loss of condition. It is almost always a result of boredom, although a horse can develop the habit by watching and copying another horse. One possible remedy is to wrap sheet metal over the top of the door. However, this is only a deterrent and it may not work. If the habit has not become established, turn the horse out into a field and he may forget about it. However, crib-biters will use the top of the gate or a fencing post to suck in air.

Crib-biting is another stable vice. The horse takes hold of the top of the door, or any suitable ledge, and sucks in air.

Wind-sucking

This is similar to crib-biting, except that the horse does not have to take hold of anything in order to swallow air. He simply arches his neck and draws in his chin. Unless you can cure the boredom, it is very difficult to cure a confirmed wind-sucker.

Some vets advocate a small operation to cure both wind-sucking and crib-biting which has been very successful. This involves making a small hole through the flesh of each cheek, which prevents the horse from creating a vacuum in his mouth.

CHAPTER 18
Feeding the stabled horse

The needs of a stabled horse are different from those of a grass-kept pony, and it is all too easy to make mistakes when you get your first horse.

When you had a pony, you could rely on his natural hardiness, his ability to do well on comparatively poor grazing, and his capacity to thrive on whatever food you chose to give him. In summer, he carried you through the season's competitions on little more than grass; in winter, his feeding programme maintained him in a healthy condition when his main source of food – the grass in his field – had little nutritional value.

A horse, however, is stabled, and you must aim to get him – and keep him – in hard condition so that he is capable of taking part in adult competitions. Hard condition, the state in which he sweats hardly at all under steady exercise, and is capable of sustained work without tiring, is achieved through the right combination of exercise and feeding. The food you give him should be energy-producing so that he can perform various tasks without distress, and his lungs should have room to expand to their full extent.

Different activities use energy in different ways. Show-jumping, eventing and polo call for sharp bursts of energy with longer periods of rest. Hunting expects sustained effort with short periods of rest.

The horse's diet, therefore, should consist of food which provides energy rather than fat, and the most usual source of energy – and the best – is oats. In the past, with your pony, you may have steered clear of oats because they can have an overheating effect on ponies. But they are an important part of a horse's diet. Horse and pony cubes can be used as a substitute for oats, but the horse would need one-and-a-half times as many cubes as oats for a feed of the same nutritional value.

Once you have worked out a suitable diet for the horse, you should stick to it as long as he is getting the exercise and work to match his intake of food. If for any reason, such as a week or two of bad weather, or the cancellation of hunting because of an outbreak of foot-and-mouth disease, the horse's work load is altered, it is important to reduce the amount of feed he is getting.

Calculate the amount of food required per day, and divide the total into three or four feeds according to your planned routine. The table opposite gives a guide to suitable amounts for different sizes of horse, but remember that it is only a guide. You should adjust the quantities according to your knowledge of your own horse.

Roots include carrots (liked by all horses), swedes, turnips, mangels and parsnips. All roots should be scrubbed under a tap and sliced in finger-shaped pieces. Some horses like to have a large root such as a swede or mangel left whole in the manger for them to chew on when they like. Chaff is included in all the above feeds because it forces the horse to chew slowly and stimulates the flow of saliva. The green food, in summer, could be lucerne, or a haynet of freshly pulled grass.

Linseed jelly is a useful addition to the feed because it improves the coat. To make linseed jelly, place about a handful in a saucepan, cover with water and leave it to soak for twenty-four hours. Then add more water and bring it to the boil. Boil vigorously for about

Winter	First feed	Second feed	Third feed	Fourth feed
	7.45 a.m.	12.30 p.m.	4.45 p.m.	7.30 p.m.
16.2 hh hunter: hunting 2–3 days a week	900 g–1.4 kg (2–3 lb) oats; 450 g (1 lb) bran; double handful chaff; 900 g (2 lb) hay	1.4 kg (3 lb) oats; 450 g (1 lb) bran; chaff; 450 g (1 lb) roots, such as carrots; 2.2 kg (5 lb) hay	1.4 kg (3 lb) oats; 450 g (1 lb) bran; chaff; 450 g (1 lb) linseed jelly	1.4–1.8 kg (3–4 lb) oats 450 g (1 lb) bran; chaff; 3.2 kg (7 lb) hay
16 hh hunter: hunting 2 days a week	900 g (2 lb) oats; 450 g (1 lb) bran; chaff; 900 g (2 lb) hay	900 g (2 lb) oats; 450 g (1 lb) bran; chaff; 450 g (1 lb) roots; 2.2 kg (5 lb) hay	900 g (2 lb) oats; 450 g (1 lb) bran; chaff; 450 g (1 lb) linseed jelly	1.4 kg (3 lb) oats; 450 g (1 lb) bran; chaff; 3.2 kg (7 lb) hay
15.2 hh hunter: hunting 1–2 days a week	450 g (1 lb) oats; 700 g (1½ lb) cubes; 450 g (1 lb) bran; chaff; 900 g (2 lb) hay	900 g (2 lb) oats; 450 g (1 lb) cubes; 450 g (1 lb) bran; chaff; 1.8 kg (4 lb) hay	900 g (2 lb) oats; 450 g (1 lb) cubes; 450 g (1 lb) bran; chaff	900 g (2 lb) oats; 1.4 kg (3 lb) cubes; 450 g (1 lb) bran; chaff; 1.8 kg (4 lb) hay

Winter	First feed	Second feed	Third feed
	7.45 a.m.	12.30 p.m.	7.30 p.m.
16.2 hh hack: daily exercise plus weekend work and occasional competition	450 g (1 lb) oats; 450 g (1 lb) cubes; 450 g (1 lb) bran; double handful chaff; 900 g (2 lb) hay	1.4 kg (3 lb) cubes; 450 g (1 lb) bran; chaff; 450 g (1 lb) roots, such as carrots 2.2 kg (5lb) hay	900 g (2 lb) oats; 450 g (1 lb) cubes; 450 g (1 lb) bran; 450 g (1 lb) flaked maize; chaff; 3.2 kg (7 lb) hay
16 hh hack: exercise as above	900 g (2 lb) cubes; 450 g (1 lb) bran; chaff; 900 g (2 lb) hay	1.4 kg (3 lb) cubes; 450 g (1 lb) bran chaff; 450 g (1 lb) roots; 2.2 kg (5 lb) hay	900 g (2 lb) oats; 450 g (1 lb) flaked maize; 450 g (1 lb) bran; chaff; 3.2 kg (7 lb) hay
15.2 hh hack: exercise as above	700 g (1½ lb) cubes; 450 g (1 lb) bran; chaff; 900 g (2 lb) hay	900 g (2 lb) cubes; 450 g (1 lb) bran; chaff; 450 g (1 lb) roots; 1.8 kg (4 lb) hay	900 g (2 lb) oats; 450 g (1 lb) flaked maize; chaff; chaff; 3.2 kg (7 lb) hay

Summer	First feed	Second feed	Third feed	Fourth feed
	7.45 a.m.	12.30 p.m.	4.30 p.m.	7.00 p.m.
16–16.2 hh show-jumper or eventer: competition work and schooling	1.4 kg (3 lb) oats; 450 g (1 lb) bran; chaff; 900 g (2 lb) hay and green food	1.4 kg (3 lb) oats; 450 g (1 lb) bran; chaff; 2.2 kg (5 lb) hay	1.8 kg (4 lb) oats; 450 g (1 lb) bran; chaff	1.8 kg (4 lb) oats; 450 g (1 lb) bran; chaff; 3.2 kg (7 lb) hay and green food
15.2 hh show hack or show-jumper	Feed as above			
15 hh polo pony or show-jumper: competition work or polo 2 days a week, and schooling	700 g (1½ lb) oats; 450 g (1 lb) bran; chaff; 900 g (2 lb) hay and green food	1.4 kg (3 lb) oats; 450 g (1 lb) bran; chaff; 2.2 kg (5 lb) hay	1.4 kg (3 lb) oats; 450 g (1 lb) bran; chaff	1.4 kg (3 lb) oats; 450 g (1 lb) bran; chaff; 2.7 kg (6 lb) hay and green food

A guide to feed quantities for different sizes of horse.

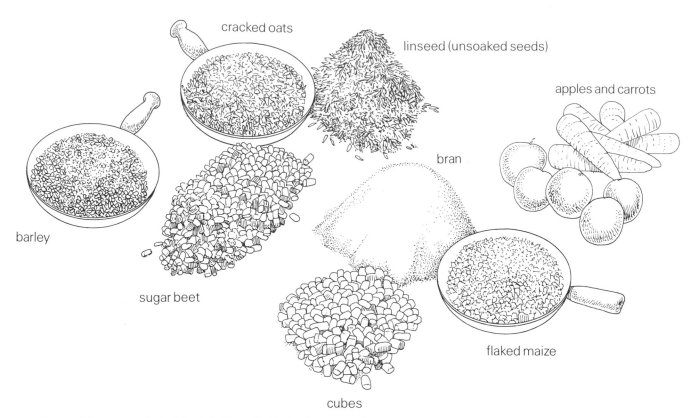

cracked oats

linseed (unsoaked seeds)

apples and carrots

bran

barley

sugar beet

flaked maize

cubes

Some of the concentrated foodstuffs available for horses and ponies

ten to fifteen minutes before taking the pan off the heat and leaving it to cool. The linseed will set as a jelly, which is then mixed with the feed. Always make certain that the linseed boils thoroughly because uncooked linseed is poisonous.

POINTS TO REMEMBER

A full feed of oats, bran, chaff, and so on, will take a horse about twenty minutes to eat and a further one and a half hours to digest. A horse should not be worked on a full stomach so always allow sufficient time between feeding and exercise. The main hay ration should be given last thing at night, when the horse has time and quiet to eat and digest it.

Always water *before* feeding.

Never leave unfinished food in the manger, because it can become sour and indigestible. In any case, the manger should be rinsed out once a day. This is easiest to do if the manger is removable. If buckets are used rather than a manger, they should be rinsed out.

Finicky feeders

Although most horses are good trenchermen, a few may be fussy, leaving half their feed in the manger. Check first that there is no identifiable cause, such as sharp teeth or stale or contaminated food. Sharp teeth may need rasping. Stale or contaminated food may be caused by bad storage, either by you or at the suppliers.

If the horse's teeth are all right and the food is perfectly acceptable to other horses, you may simply have a fuss-pot on your hands. The solution is to try alternative foodstuffs: flaked maize instead of oats, beans instead of cubes. Molasses, unrefined sugar which looks rather like treacle, is excellent for tempting horses to eat. A spoonful should be mixed with warm water and sprinkled on the food. Black treacle could be tried instead. Or add raw eggs or stout to the feed.

Some horses do not have big appetites, and the amount of food given at each feed-time may be too much. Try dividing the day's ration into six or seven smaller feeds. If all else fails, try cutting out the short feed altogether for a day, although making sure that the horse has plenty of hay and fresh water. A short period of starvation can do wonders in persuading a delicate feeder to eat.

It is worth taking time and trouble to find

the reason for the lack of enthusiasm at feed-time and to discover a cure. A shy feeder is difficult to get into condition.

Poor doers

Here, you have a similar problem, but it may be more difficult to solve. A poor doer usually eats well, but fails to put on weight, tending to look thin and under-nourished. Provided his skinny look is not due to bad conforma-tion, such as a long back with too great a space between ribs and pelvis, search for the cause and do your best to eliminate it.

Start by examining the worming pro-gramme you have been using with the horse. How effective is it? Does he need worming more often? If necessary, consult the vet.

If you are satisfied that he is being wormed often enough and laboratory tests do not reveal a massive infestation, check his teeth. Does he dribble food from his mouth while eating, a condition known as quidding? Over-sharp teeth are a likely cause. Sharp teeth may also inhibit proper mastication so that the food is being swallowed before it has been properly pre-digested. This will prevent a horse from getting sufficient nourishment from the food.

Vary the diet. Perhaps your horse is not getting enough of the right kind of food. It may be worth increasing his hay ration because some horses need more fibre in their diet than others. Check the quality of the food.

Watch your horse to see how he eats his food. If he is very greedy, he may be swallow-ing his food too quickly. The solution to this is to add extra chaff to his feed to encourage him to chew more slowly.

Change his water bucket more frequently. He may not be drinking enough; either because the water is stale, or because he likes to rinse his mouth out while feeding and by dribbling food into the bucket is contaminat-ing the water.

If none of these suggestions applies to your horse, you may find that the reason lies in his temperament. Is he a nervy animal, always breaking out into a sweat? Does he walk round and round his box? Nervy horses may need a soothing companion such as an elderly pony, a goat or even a stable cat. Or perhaps he needs to be turned out into a paddock for a short time each day. If this is the case, you should arrange to give him an hour or two of feedom. In winter leave him in the paddock in a New Zealand rug. In summer, turn him out at night (when there are no flies around) and bring him in during the daylight hours.

HORSES AT REST

Even the most dedicated rider likes to take a holiday sometimes. Holidays from school, college or work may be just the opportunity you want in order to spend more time with your horse, but there are other leisure activi-ties in life and your family could be very pleased if you decided to spend a holiday with them.

Clearly, you cannot simply abandon your horse for a fortnight while you are away. For most people, the answer lies in the services of a friend who is willing, in return for riding your horse, to look after him in exactly the same way as you would do. That is the simpl-est solution and has the advantage that your horse suffers no break in his regular routine.

Alternatively, you could send the horse to livery while you are away. This has disadvan-tages, the main one being that he is taken away from his familiar surroundings, put in a strange stable, and his routine will have to fit into the one practised by the livery stables, which may, of course, be totally different from your own. Even though your absence may be no longer than two or three weeks, it will still take time for your horse to settle down again once he comes home.

Some people, especially those for whom hunting is the main interest, choose to turn their horses out to grass for two or three months in the summer and then take their own holiday during that time. If you do this, you will still need someone to keep an eye on your horse when you are away, but it will be a less arduous task than looking after him in the stable would be.

If you regularly rest your horse in the sum-mer, it is sensible to prepare him gradually, a process known as *roughing off*. Start by cutting out his hard food, reducing his exercise and giving him a bran mash every day for a few days. At the same time, take him out to graze for an hour or two each day so that his diges-tion can adjust to the change. He will then be able to make the transition to a full grass diet without any problems arising.

Before turning him out, you should have his shoes removed and his feet trimmed. If he has good hard feet with no cracking or split-ting of the hoof, he can safely run out without shoes. If not, have his feet fitted with thin half-shoes, known as grass-tips, which are worn on the front of the hooves to protect the wall of the hoof near the toe.

As well as the usual requirements in a field, such as safe fencing and an ample supply of fresh water, there should be a field shelter, where the horse can stand out of the hot sun and escape from the flies.

Most horses benefit from some light riding while at grass. Quite apart from giving them a change of scene, the exercise will make it easier to get them back into condition as the working season approaches.

Show-jumpers are sometimes rested during the winter. Usually, this means turning them out during the day and bringing them in at night. As with horses that are rested in the summer, they will need only a light diet while they are on holiday. High-energy foods, such as oats, should be cut out altogether and boiled barley or soaked sugar-beet pulp should be substituted.

CONDITIONING FOR WORK

While at grass, a horse becomes soft and fat. His muscles grow flabby and his belly takes up more space, pressing on his chest and restricting his lungs. Before he can be put back into work, he has to be hardened off, his muscles built up and his fatness reduced so that his lungs can expand to their full extent.

The method of conditioning your horse for work depends on how long he has been at grass, how much food he has received other than grass, and whether he has been ridden at all during that time. Whatever his state, you should allow plenty of time – at least six weeks and preferably twelve – before he is capable of working hard without distress.

Start by worming the horse, and have his teeth inspected and, if necessary, rasped. Ask the farrier to remove the grass-tips, tidy his feet and shoe him. Bring him into the stable for longer periods each day.

Unless you have been giving him regular exercise while he was at grass, you should confine your riding for the first three weeks to walking only, starting with about twenty to twenty-five minutes each day and working up to one-and-a-half hours.

Gradually introduce some slow trotting, and increase the exercise time to two-and-a-half to three hours. Try to include plenty of uphill work, to build up the muscles of his quarters and improve his wind. As the soft belly fatness disappears, his lungs will have more room to expand, and he will sweat less easily.

Throughout this period, slowly increase the amount of hard food in the horse's diet until, by the time he is required to start work again, he will be back on his full ration.

If he has not been ridden at all during the summer, it is important to watch out for girth galls and saddle sores. To harden the skin, the back and girth area may be sponged with a salt-water solution.

Some roadwork may be beneficial as a means of hardening the legs, but be careful not to overdo it.

CHAPTER 19
Careers with horses

When you have owned a horse for a year or two, you will know whether riding for you is always going to be just a hobby, or whether you would like to earn a living working with horses.

Many young people go through a stage of wanting to work with horses. For most, it is never more than a stage. Other interests gradually take over until eventually they give up riding altogether. They never lose their

Working with horses demands the qualities of patience and calmness, together with physical courage and strength. Here the horse is being lunged, which improves suppleness and teaches obedience.

love of horses, of course, and are likely to become involved again when their own children are old enough to enjoy ponies, but for the time being horses take a back seat.

If, however, you are seriously interested in working with horses, you should first examine the different careers available, finding out what qualifications are required, what the work involves and how you can best prepare yourself to enter the profession. You should also examine your own character as honestly as you can.

PERSONAL QUALITIES

Working with any animal requires patience, calmness, kindness and a highly developed sense of responsibility. Working with horses may also require physical courage.

Ask yourself various questions. Are you the type who gets in a flap when things go wrong? Can you be firm when necessary? Do you mind working at all hours? Will you cheerfully turn out when the weather is wet and windy?

Another requirement is that you should be physically healthy and reasonably strong. There is nothing like lugging a few bales of hay about or raking over the surface of an all-weather school to leave you feeling wrung out and ready to drop. It is even worse when you know that you still have half a dozen horses to muck out, feed and get ready for the night.

Hard work is part of any career with horses. Even if you become a top show-jumper, life will not consist just of being a superstar at Wembley, handing your horse to a groom and signing countless autographs. Even the top show-jumpers spend a great deal of time training, bringing on young horses and, probably most tedious of all, travelling.

Nevertheless, there is a great deal of satisfaction to be had from working with horses and sometimes good financial rewards as well. There are also many different ways to make a living on the equestrian scene.

RIDING INSTRUCTOR

In order to teach riding, a person must hold one of the British Horse Society's qualifying certificates, which are awarded to students passing the relevant examinations. These qualifications are: the Assistant Instructor's, which entitles the holder to put the letters BHSAI after their name; the Intermediate Instructor's (BHSII); the Instructor's (BHSI); and the Fellowship of the British Horse Society (FBHS). There is a minimum age limit for each examination: seventeen-and-a-half years for the BHSAI, twenty-two years for the BHSI, and twenty-five years for the Fellowship. Minimum entry requirements for the courses leading to these examinations are four GCSE passes except for those who are twenty years or over at the time they start the course.

Because the British Horse Society is recognized as a responsible body for setting and maintaining standards of riding and teaching, further education grants may be available from county educational authorities for any student wishing to enrol on a course.

Training may take place at any recognized establishment and can be done either as a working pupil or as a fee-paying student. Training usually lasts a year in the case of a working pupil, sometimes less when the tuition is paid for.

GROOM

A groom may be solely responsible for looking after someone's horses, or be part of a large stable. He or she should, of course, know all about horse management and be able to exercise many different horses. They should know how to get a horse fit, and how to prepare him for a show. In addition, it helps to be able to drive.

A groom's work can be very hard and is often poorly paid. Unscrupulous employers rely on their grooms' dedication to the horses in their care and are not above exploiting them quite shamelessly. A good employer, however, can make a groom's life extremely pleasant. For example, to work for a leading show-jumper or eventer can provide a life of constant variety and excitement.

The BHS Horsemastership examination or the Groom's Diploma offered by the Association of British Riding Schools provides the paper qualifications necessary to be a groom. For the former, the syllabus is the same as that laid down for the BHSAI, but without the teaching. For the latter, a minimum of eighteen months' full-time work with horses is required, and the entrant must be at least seventeen-and-a-half years old when taking the examination. The Groom's Diploma is recognized in most countries as evidence of competence.

The BHS also offers a Stable Manager's

Certificate, which qualifies the holder to manage or own any kind of yard, and to train student grooms. Preparation for this certificate also covers the business side of stable management.

RACING

There are two types of racing; flat racing and National Hunt racing. The latter takes place over jumps; either steeplechase jumps or hurdles. In the UK, both flat racing and National Hunt racing are under the control of the Jockey Club. The most valuable horses, and the greatest prizes and prestige, are found in flat racing.

In both cases, racehorses are kept at training establishments, where they are looked after by 'lads', who in many cases are actually 'lasses'. A lad is a lad whatever his or her age, from a youngster just out of school up to the Head Lad, who is quite possibly a grandparent.

Lads are the stable staff, who are responsible for the feeding, grooming and mucking-out of the horses in their care. They may or may not ride the horses out to exercise, depending on their own wishes and the policy of the individual trainer.

Aspiring flat jockeys are called apprentices. They are contracted to stay with a particular stable for three, five or seven years. Like the lads, apprentices 'do' two or three horses in the yard, looking after them entirely themselves, riding them out to exercise and travelling with them when they go racing.

An apprentice might not ride in an actual race for as much as a year after joining a stable. Flat meetings often have special races for apprentices, and that may be the first opportunity to don proper silks and appear in public on a real racecourse. However, an apprentice who is a particularly good rider may be entered in other races, especially if, by doing so, the trainer can claim a weight allowance. Racehorses carry a stipulated weight according to their ability. Obviously, the more weight a horse has to carry, the greater his disadvantage over other horses in a race. However, a young jockey's inexperience is counter-balanced by the fact that his or her mount carries less weight. If an apprentice wins a few races, the allowance is reduced accordingly, until eventually no allowance at all is given.

In a flat-racing training stables, the horses will be much younger than those found in a National Hunt stables. Horses are allowed to start racing at two years old, and many trainers break in young horses when they are about eighteen months old. Apprentices who are very light, small-boned but strong, may well be asked to help with the breaking in, and will be taught how to lunge and to back young horses.

Many National Hunt horses began with flat racing, and later switched to jumping. Consistent winners on the flat are usually retired to stud by the age of four or five years. However, some of the less brilliant ones will be tried over hurdles and later perhaps steeplechase fences, especially if they show stamina rather than speed.

The financial rewards for leading flat jockeys are very great indeed, but only about one in ten apprentices manages to become a jockey, and of these only a very few reach the top.

But a lad's work can be satisfying, especially for those who take pride in turning out a horse at the peak of fitness and appearance. Most lads become very attached to the horses in their care – and vice versa – and nowhere are patience, understanding, and gentleness more valuable than in dealing with skittish young Thoroughbreds.

STUD WORK

This is one of the most rewarding careers, and it is extremely important work. Good handling of a foal is absolutely vital to producing a kind temperament in the adult horse. A horse's life-long attitude to human beings depends on its early introduction to the way in which human beings behave. Patience allied to firmness is essential in anyone dealing with brood mares and their offspring.

The National Pony Society offers a Stud Assistant's Certificate, followed by a Diploma in stud work. Both are awarded as a result of fairly stiff practical examinations. Trainees at a stud learn how to manage, handle and look

Page 172 A farrier at work. A farrier's job is highly skilled; it requires knowledge not only of how to make and put on shoes, but also of the horses movement, the ways in which shoeing can correct faulty action and balance, and of diseases of the foot. The training involves a four-year apprenticeship.
Page 173 The training for a veterinary surgeon lasts for five years. A vet who wishes to work with horses will need to practise in an area with a large equine population. A veterinary training can also lead on to working in equine research.

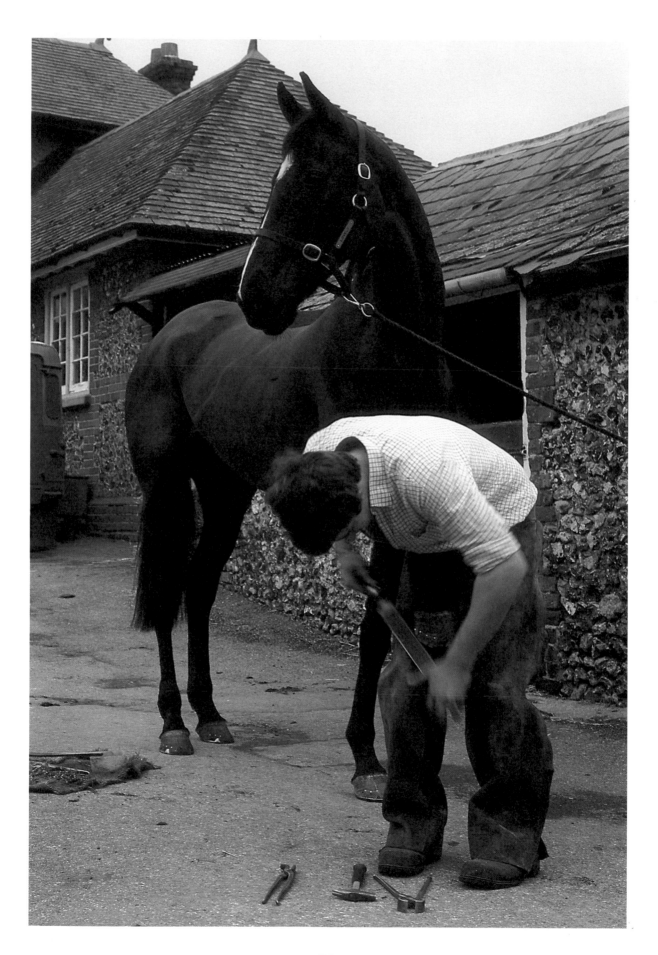

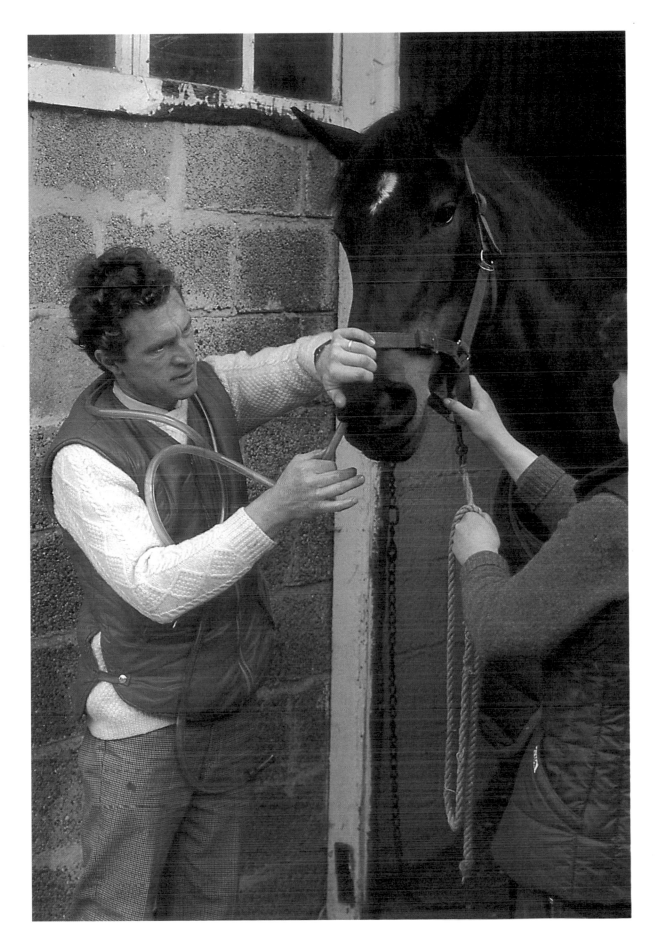

after stallions and brood mares; and about the feeding and weaning of foals. They are taught how to handle young ponies, and how to lunge and back them; how to prepare for and present animals in the show-ring; and how to train young horses under the saddle.

Someone who is interested in bloodstock breeding – that is, the breeding and raising of Thoroughbreds – should seek advice from the Thoroughbred Breeders' Association as to which studs are willing to accept students.

HUNT SERVICE

Anyone who enjoys hunting tends to think of it as a sport to be paid for, and forgets that there are people who earn their livelihood in the hunting world. The principal employee of a hunt is the Huntsman, who, quite apart from hunting hounds, is in charge of the hunt stables and the hunt kennels. The Kennel Huntsman looks after the field when the Master is not hunting, and is answerable to the Huntsman. Whippers-in may be amateurs, but most are paid employees and the positions of First Whipper-in and Second Whipper-in represent stepping stones on the way to becoming a huntsman. Under the Second Whipper-in is the Second Horseman, who takes charge of the hunt horses at a meet, while under him are the various grooms and stable boys employed in the stables.

This type of job is definitely for the country-lover, and for someone who has the patience and love of animals that any work with horses requires. In addition, hunt servants need tact when dealing with people: they are ambassadors for the hunt whenever they appear in public, and must be able to keep their tempers even when provoked.

Openings in hunt work are clearly limited in number. There is no examination, and no official qualification. A visit to the local kennels for a chat with the huntsman may be the best means of starting in this type of work. If there are no openings locally, the huntsman may know of vacancies in other hunts.

FARRIER

The farrier is the one person with whom every horse-owner is likely to get acquainted. You will have visited the farrier – or the farrier you – at least six times a year ever since you acquired your first pony. You may have had more than one farrier during that time, and if you held your pony each time his feet were attended to, you will have had plenty of opportunity to watch a farrier at work.

The farrier is one of the most important people in a horse's life. Without the knowledge and skill they bring to their work, a horse would be incapable of carrying out the tasks expected of him. A careless farrier can lame a horse for life. Badly-fitted shoes, incorrectly trimmed feet, or nails driven home without thought, can all make a horse unsound. Think of the weight that a horse's feet have to bear; in some activities, such as jumping or galloping, there is a moment when all that weight is carried by one foot alone.

There was a time when every village had its forge. When machines replaced horses on the roads and in agriculture, the farrier's profession declined. But the growing popularity of riding for leisure increased the demand again, and although the village smithy has not made a comeback the farrier certainly has.

Modern farriers are much more mobile than their predecessors. They still need a forge, complete with fire and anvil, in which to make shoes, but it is no longer essential for them to shoe horses alongside it. Now, they carry their tools with them and travel to their clients by car. If hot shoeing is required, they may have a portable forge, but many farriers offer only a cold shoeing service and still have more customers than they can deal with.

Farriers need to know more than how to make shoes and to put them on. They must understand the way a horse's limbs work, especially the tendons and joints, and how they are affected by the shape of the hoof. They must know about diseases of the foot and the remedies that they can apply. They must be aware of what they can do to correct faulty action or to improve a horse's balance.

With so much knowledge needed, it follows that training takes a long time. It involves being apprenticed to a master farrier for four years, and attending courses, during this time, in farriery at special schools approved by the Worshipful Company of Farriers. At the end of this training, there is an examination; and those who are successful become Registered Shoeing Smiths and can set up in business. Later on, further qualifications can be added; by becoming an Associate of the Farriery Company of London, or a Fellow of the Worshipful Company of Farriers.

VETERINARY SURGEON

A vet's training takes as long as that of a doctor: five years at any of the six veterinary colleges in the UK. At least three good A-level passes in scientific subjects are needed to win a place, and competiton is very keen.

The training includes a certain amount of practical work; such as working on a farm and, in the three years before the final examinations, as a student in a veterinary practice. The course leads to a bachelor's degree, Bachelor of Veterinary Medicine and Surgery, (BVMS), and then to Membership of the Royal College of Veterinary Surgeons (MRCVS). Post-graduate work can lead to doctorates in veterinary medicine and surgery, and to a Fellowship of the Royal College (FRCVS).

A newly-qualified vet may join an existing practice; first as an assistant, and later, if good enough, as a partner. On the other hand, some people prefer to go into veterinary research, or to enter the civil service and work for the Ministry of Agriculture.

There can be no guarantee, of course, that a vet's work will include horses, although they are bound to be among the patients of a country practice. Those who prefer to deal with horses rather than other animals, should try to join a practice in an area with a large equine population; if possible, one that includes several racing stables. It may be possible eventually to build up a reputation as an equine specialist whose services are greatly in demand; but no one can say at the start of their training that they wish to deal with horses alone.

Those whose interest lies in research should aim to work, eventually, for the Newmarket Equine Research Station, where all manner of horse diseases and problems are investigated.

VETERINARY NURSE

Those who wish to have a career caring for sick animals, but do not have the necessary qualifications to train as a veterinary surgeon, can join the veterinary profession as a nurse, becoming a Registered Animal Nursing Auxiliary (RANA). Nurses, like veterinary surgeons, cannot opt to work just with horses.

RANA trainees must be at least seventeen years old when they start, and will need three O-levels; in English, and either mathematics or physical or biological science. The training consists of working as a nurse with a professional veterinary surgeon, and attending lectures at college when required. Courses include animal anatomy and physiology; and anaesthesia, so that the nurse can assist a veterinary surgeon during an operation.

OTHER WORK CONNECTED WITH HORSES

If none of the jobs so far mentioned interests you sufficiently, but you would still like a career connected with horses, you might like to work in a saddlers. All over the country, there are numerous saddlery shops where a young assistant can gain a great deal of satisfaction from selling tack and other equipment. Many of these shops take their goods in mobile vans around to the shows; even quite small shows have a number of trade stands these days.

With a certain amount of capital behind you, you could even start up on your own, although it would be wise to work for a time in someone else's shop first, to learn the business and get to know the representatives of the various manufacturers.

If you are interested in saddlery, you could seek an apprenticeship with a Master Saddler, where for a period of about five years you would learn the craft of leather-working and saddle-making.

Another field in which a knowledge of horses and riding can provide a good living is in buying and selling horses. The most important quality in this work is honesty. A dealer's reputation goes before him and the surest road to ruin is to attribute non-existent virtues to a horse in order to make a quick sale. However, dealers who do their best to find a suitable animal for a client, and who can tell, better than the client can, what exactly he or she wants, are always in great demand.

Pages 176–77 An instructor at work: holding the pony of a young pupil, while he mounts unaided.

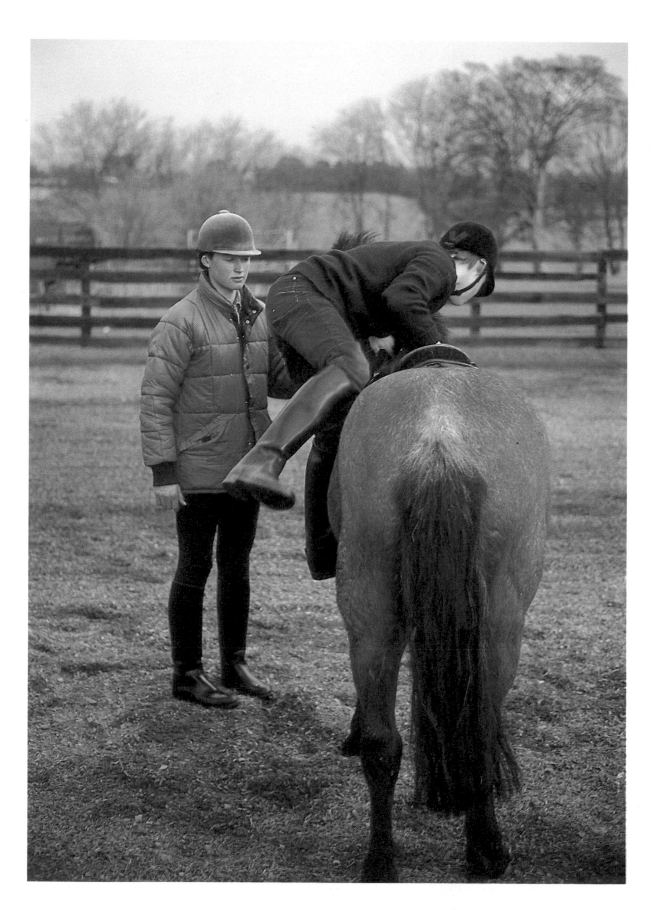

Appendices

APPENDIX I
Mainly for parents

From the moment you become a pony-owner to the time you have grown up, your parents will be your partners in the pony-owning venture. Even if they know nothing at all about horses at the outset, they will over the years become very knowledgeable, because there is no way in which they can avoid being involved. This section gives them some idea of what they are getting involved in.

At the beginning, a parent's involvement is principally financial. It is unrealistic to expect any child to be able to pay the costs of looking after a pony all by herself. Even if you own a field, the upkeep of a pony can run into several pounds a week.

The cost is not spread evenly throughout the year. In summer, when a pony is feeding almost solely on grass, he is cheap to keep. In winter, hay and concentrates soon run up big bills at the corn-chandlers. Shoeing expenses crop up every eight weeks or so, and veterinary bills – even for routine things like worming powders and anti-tetanus and anti-flu vaccinations – add to the annual cost.

You can be sure that, whatever a pony has – in the way of saddlery, grooming kits, clothing, and so on – his young owner will always think that he needs more. Anti-sweat rugs, summer sheets, tail bandages, leg bandages, travelling bandages, tail guards, rubber reins, drop nosebands, grooming kit boxes, buckets, haynets, fly fringes; the list never gets any shorter. Hoof-picks are forever getting lost and have to be replaced; saddles need re-stuffing from time to time; whips vanish into thin air.

The rider grows and needs new clothes: jodhpur boots fall apart, one pair of jodhpurs is superseded by two, three, even four or five pairs, a tweed jacket is joined by a showing jacket.

The Pony Club subscription comes up once a year. Show entry fees, which are quite small while the rider is still on the leading rein, get more expensive as pony and rider progress to bigger and better competitions.

Competitions, in turn, lead to even more expense. The velvet-covered riding hat is fine for gymkhanas, but once a child starts entering Pony Club events, she will need a proper crash hat, and for cross-country riding a back protector and a rugby shirt in her chosen colours.

INSURANCE

A pony is a valuable animal; it is also a living creature subject to illness and accidents, sometimes fatal. It should be regarded as an investment, and protected as such.

There are a number of insurance policies on the market, advertised in the horse magazines. All that is necessary is to choose the most suitable, fill in the proposal form on the advertisement, enclose a cheque for the premium, and post it off. Alternatively, insurance can be arranged through a broker.

Policies are usually graded to cater for different needs. Basic insurance will provide cover against loss or injury incurred during ordinary hacking and Pony Club events. Some activities, such as hunting, attract higher premiums. There are clauses covering veterinary fees, permanent disablement of the animal, and theft of the pony. Saddlery can be covered. And a trailer can be insured for a small extra premium. Personal liability is included in all policies. This provides cover against claims arising from injury to a third party caused by your pony. Most policies have an excess clause.

TRAILERS

Once a child regularly takes part in competitions, the question of whether to buy a trailer or horse-box will arise.

In the past, it was quite usual for young competitors to attend all the shows within a 12-mile radius of their homes without using a horse-box. Today however, motorways and busy roads have made hacking any distance a risky business. And it is unreasonable to expect a keenly competitive child to be content with the few shows which are close enough to be reached on horseback.

It may be possible to beg a lift from time to time in someone else's trailer, but friends, however obliging, may not always be going to the same event. Even if they are, your classes and theirs may not coincide. One or other of you will be kept hanging about, either having to arrive too early or leave too late. It is possible to hire a trailer, but sooner or later, you will probably decide to buy one.

Always buy the best trailer you can afford. Trailers range in size from those which can take two ponies, to those big enough for two 17.2 hh horses. Single-sized trailers are available, but most horses and ponies travel better with a companion, and to take someone else's pony in your trailer will add very little to the expense.

A trailer with a front-unload (that is, fitted with a front ramp as well as a rear one) is heavier than one with a rear ramp only. On the other hand, it is easier and safer to lead a horse forwards out of the trailer than to back him down a rear ramp. It is also easier to get a shy loader into a front-unload trailer.

The floor is particularly important as this is the part which is likely to rot. It should be made of hardwood, preferably with a 3 mm (⅛ in) gap between the planks so that urine can drain easily and air can circulate to speed up the drying. The lighting system should work properly; side and tail-lights, braking lights and indicators are operated from the towing vehicle. If possible have the wheel bearings examined.

A double-axle trailer is more stable than one with only a single axle. Inspect the tyres carefully, especially the tyre walls. Since a trailer often spends more time parked than in use, the tyre treads are likely to wear less quickly than the tyre walls.

Inside, most trailers have padding on the side walls and a central, removable partition, which may be no more than a single bar secured fore and aft by a vertical pillar. Partitions which reach to the floor should be padded. There are usually detachable breast bars and jockey straps.

Some trailers are fitted with non-slip matting on the ramps, which deadens the sound as the pony is being loaded.

Second-hand trailers are advertised regularly in magazines and local papers. If you buy a second-hand trailer, the points to look at are the condition of the floor; the state of the lighting system; the ease of raising and lowering the ramps; the brakes and wheels. If possible, have the trailer examined by an expert before buying it.

TOWING VEHICLES

Most trailers can be towed quite easily by a family car with an engine capacity of 2,000 cc. A tow-bar will be needed on the car. Four-wheel drive vehicles are at an advantage in wet weather conditions.

TOWING A TRAILER

Of all the duties that a pony-owning parent is expected to fulfil, to tow a trailer with horses inside is the one which causes the most apprehension. Yet many do so regularly without mishap.

If you have never towed a trailer before, start by taking it out on the road when it is empty. An empty trailer is not exactly like a full one, but it will give you an idea of how your car behaves with a trailer behind it and you can practise starting, stopping, and

Pages 180–81 Loading. A pony is more willing to follow if the handler walks quietly into the box without looking at him. This pony has confidence, but difficult loaders may be cured of their problems if a front unload trailer is used and the front ramp lowered. Coconut matting on the loading ramps will help to deaden noise.

turning corners without having to worry about any passengers.

Practise reversing as well. This can cause all sorts of difficulties, so it is wise to master the technique as soon as possible. It may help to have a look at the way a toy Land-Rover and trailer work, provided the toy has movable front wheels operated by the steering wheel. It will show you exactly what the trailer does when you steer the towing vehicle. The trailer acts in an opposite fashion to the car. In other words, if you wish the trailer to bend to the right, you turn the car's steering wheel to the left, reversing the wheel only when the movement has been established. Try it out a few times with the toy trailer on the carpet.

Once on the road with a loaded trailer, you should aim to give the occupants as smooth a ride as possible. This means early anticipation of changes of direction and speed. Remember that your stopping distances are increased by the weight of the trailer, and start changing to a lower gear well before you reach a road junction so that you can come to a stop without any unnecessary jerk. You should also move off as smoothly as possible, taking time to go through the gears.

Take corners slightly wider than you would if you were driving the car by itself, to allow for the extra width of the trailers, and at crossroads bear in mind the extra length of car and trailer combined.

If you are taking only one horse or pony in a double trailer, the animal will have a better journey if he is loaded into the right-hand side. With two ponies of different sizes, travel with the bigger one on the outside.

The speed at which you travel depends on the nature of the road. Although 50 mph (80 km/h) is the legal limit, it is better to keep the speed to a maximum of 40 mph (64 km/h). The time lost on a journey of 10 miles (16 km) is only a few minutes, and it is better to set off early and arrive with a pair of calm ponies, than to drive as fast as possible thereby flustering the ponies.

Finally, remember other road-users. There is nothing more frustrating for other drivers than to be stuck behind a trailer with no hope of passing it safely. So if you are on a narrow road and the traffic behind you is building up, pull into a lay-by when you see one and allow the cars to pass. You will waste only a minute or two at the most, but you will be making a worthwhile contribution to road safety.

LOADING AND UNLOADING A PONY

A horse or pony which walks quietly into a trailer first time, with no fuss, is a joy to own. Most ponies load quite willingly, but there are always a few who, through sheer naughtiness, like to make a fuss.

If this is the case with your horse, and as long as you are satisfied that the animal is not frightened, you have to be firm. Often, just the production of a lunge-line or whip will do the trick. A lunge-line is connected to one side of the trailer ramp, brought round to the other side behind the horse and gradually tightened around his hindquarters. Coupled with a firm leader at the animal's head, the extra pressure should be sufficient to persuade him to enter the trailer.

If this fails because the horse swings his rear end off the trailer ramp, you will need extra help. Two lunge-lines crossed behind his quarters, with a strong person on each end, may provide the necessary compulsion. A further line, clipped to his headcollar and passing through a ring inside the trailer at the front, with the free end coming back out of the trailer alongside the horse, where a third assistant can apply steady pressure, is the next method to try.

Sometimes a horse just likes to take his time. If he likes to stand still and take a look around between each step, you will have to allow him to do this. Any sign of impatience will build up his resistance, whereas left to himself, he will probably walk quietly into the trailer eventually. You will just have to allow as much time as is needed before each journey. Greedy animals may be tempted into a trailer by the offer of food; other horses will load only if their companion has entered first. In every case, get to know your horse in order to find the best way of tackling any problem.

If your trailer has a front ramp it is quite simple to unload the horse. The handler gets into the trailer and removes the front bar. As soon as she is ready, the assistant outside lowers the ramp and the pony is led forwards from the trailer. When lowering the ramp, stand slightly to one side to avoid being knocked down or injured if the pony decides to make his exit at a run.

Unloading backwards is slightly more hazardous, as the jockey strap under the horse's hindquarters cannot be undone until the ramp is down. If a horse always rushes out very quickly, it is best not to use the jockey strap at all.

The handler should always talk to the horse in a soothing way, whether the animal is being unloaded frontwards or backwards.

PARTING WITH A PONY

At various stages through your child's riding career, you will be faced with the distress caused by parting with a much-loved pony. It is best if the old pony goes while the child is at school. There is bound to be a certain amount of grief, but excitement over the replacement will soon ease the pain. The process is easier when you already have a new pony to take the place of the previous one.

However, the main concern at this time is the question of finding a good home for the pony. If you can inspect his new premises and meet the family of the new owner, your fears should be allayed. But, of course, once you have actually accepted a cheque for the pony, he is no longer your responsibility. You cannot object because his new way of life is different from the one he had with you. However, if you discover that he is being ill-treated, you should contact the police or an animal welfare organization.

Many people decide to put a much-loved pony out on loan. With a little forethought, this type of transaction can be very successful. The advantage is that you still retain some control over the pony; and if the new home proves successful the loan might eventually lead to a sale. However, do make certain that your loan agreement covers every contingency, and that both parties fully understand what they have agreed to verbally. It is best to put all the conditions of the loan down in writing and to prepare two copies of the agreement, which are then signed by both parties.

Points to settle are the length of the loan; whether the loan is to include tack and other equipment; who is to be responsible for insuring the pony; paying for his feed, shoeing and veterinary bills. Discuss who makes the decision if, for any reason, the pony has to be humanely destroyed. If you trust the other family, it is better to leave this to them; a pony should not have to suffer unnecessarily because you are away when the decision has to be made.

A PARENT'S INVOLVEMENT

It is inevitable that your child's interest in riding will involve you increasingly as she gets older, even if you have no previous experience of horses. Many parents find that their lives and leisure take on a new dimension when their children take to riding. There are so many ways in which parents can become involved; supervising the care of the pony, driving to and from shows, building show-jumps for the paddock at home, and helping in the organization of the local branch of the Pony Club. Some parents dread the day that their children finally give up riding, but the Pony Club does provide them with the opportunity for continued involvement with horses long after their children have grown up.

APPENDIX II
The Pony Club

All young riders, whatever their ability, are well advised to join the Pony Club. This is an organization for children and teenagers, up to the age of twenty-one. It has helped and encouraged many thousands of young pony riders, including many well-known riders who have reached the top of their profession.

The Pony Club was formed in 1929 in the UK, where there are more than 350 branches, with a further 1,500 branches or affiliated clubs in other parts of the world.

Each branch is run by voluntary helpers, headed by a District Commissioner, and organizes a variety of riding activities, both instructional and competitive. These include working rallies, where instruction is given according to a rider's ability; competitions with neighbouring branches; outings to major horse shows; and other activities such as scavenger hunts, quizzes, barbecues and discos.

Most branches run an annual camp where, in addition to learning about pony care and management, members have the chance to train in various competitive forms of riding, such as show-jumping, gymkhana games, cross-country and dressage. Some branches also run teams for specialized events such as tetrathlon (riding, running, swimming and shooting) and polo.

All instruction at working rallies and camps is given by trained instructors. To ensure that good riding standards are maintained, members may take tests, the easiest of which is the D test, and the hardest the A test. Very few reach the latter standard, and those who do usually go on to a career with horses.

The annual subscription is not high, and all young riders derive some benefit from membership, if only the opportunity to make friends among people with the same interests. It also provides access to adults with experience and knowledge of ponies and horses, whose advice you will almost certainly need from time to time.

If you do not know who runs the Pony Club in your area, you should write to the national headquarters (see Address List), who will be able to give you the name and address of your nearest branch.

APPENDIX III
Standard abbreviations used in advertisements

SJ	Show-jumping.
CC or XC	Cross-country.
CT	Combined training.
WHP	Working hunter pony – generally applies to a pony which has been placed in WHP classes. This means that it can clear a course of rustic fences and also has good conformation.
PC	Pony Club.
RC	Riding Club.
PBA	Ponies of Britain Association – the pony is registered with the Association. It suggests a nice-looking pony of mountain and moorland type.
NPS	National Pony Society – as above.
BSPS	British Show Pony Society – the pony has quality and is probably a good candidate for showing classes.
M/M	Mountain and moorland – the pony is a native pony, probably registered with one of the breed societies.
HT	Hunter trials or horse trials.
ODE	One-day event.
TB	Thoroughbred – usually refers to a part-bred or cross-bred (i.e., the pony has Thoroughbred blood).
PoB or POB	Ponies of Britain – usually indicates that the pony has qualified for the Ponies of Britain show at Peterborough (the mecca for showing ponies of all kinds).
BSJA	British Show Jumping Association.
JC	Junior Grade 'C' – one of the BSJA grades. Ponies which jump in affiliated jumping classes have to be registered with the BSJA and be the property of members of the BSJA. Affiliated jumping classes have courses of a certain height which ponies must complete within a specific time limit. Once JC ponies have won a particular amount of prize-money, they are upgraded and can only enter show-jumping competitions open to that grade.
JA	Junior Grade 'A' – the top grade in BSJA jumping ponies.
BHS	British Horse Society.
HIS	Hunter Improvement Society – a society aimed at improving the quality of hunters.
HOYS	Horse of the Year Show – the major show in London, which marks the climax of the season and takes place at Wembley every October.
Sec. A/B/C/D	Registered divisions of the Welsh Pony Society. Section A: limited to mountain ponies not over 12 hh. Section B: ponies 12 to 13.2 hh. Section C: Welsh ponies of cob type. Section D: Welsh cobs.

APPENDIX IV
Address list

Britain

Association of British Riding Schools
Chesham House
56 Green End Road
Sawtry
Huntingdon
Cambridgeshire PE17 5UY

British Horse Society *and*
British Show Jumping Association *and*
The Pony Club
British Equestrian Centre
Kenilworth
Warwickshire CV8 2LR

British Show Pony Society
The Croft House
East Road
Oundle
Peterborough
Northamptonshire

Byeways and Bridleways Trust
9 Queen Anne's Gate
Westminster
London SW1

English Riding Holidays and
Trekking Association
Homestead Farm
Charlton Musgrave
Wincanton
Somerset

Horse Rangers Association
The Royal Mews
Hampton Court Palace
East Molesey
Surrey

International League for the Protection
of Horses
67a Camden High Street
London NW1

Irish Horse Board
St Maelruans
Tallaght
County Dublin
Ireland

National Pony Society
Cross-and-Pillory Lane
Alton
Hampshire

Ponies of Britain
Ascot Racecourse
Berkshire

The Pony Club
British Equestrian Centre
Kenilworth
Warwickshire CV8 2LR

Riding for the Disabled Association
Avenue R
National Agricultural Centre
Kenilworth
Warwickshire CV8 2LZ

United States

American Association of Sheriff Posses and
Riding Clubs
8133-B White Settlement Road
Fort Worth
TX 76108

American Horse Council
1700 K Street NW
Washington
DC 20006

American Horse Protection Association
1312 18th Street NW
Washinggton
DC 20036

American Horse Shows Association
598 Madison Avenue
New York
NY 10022

Pony of the Americas Club Inc
PO Box 1447
Mason City
IA 50401

United States Pony Clubs
303 High Street
West Chester
PA 19380

Canada
Canadian Equestrian Federation
333 River Road
Vanier
ON K1L 8B9

Canadian Pony Society
387 Hay Street
Woodstock
ON N4S 2C5

Australia
Australian Riding Pony Association
Seymour Road
Nar Nar Goon
Victoria

Pony Clubs Association of Western Australia
13 Violet Gardens
Shenton Park
WA 6008

South Australia Horse Society
Fisher Road
Hahndorf
SA 5245

Western Australia Horsemen's Association
50 Bombard Street
Mount Pleasant
WA 6153

South Africa
South African National Equestrian Federation
PO Box 52365
Saxonwold 2132

Index

Page numbers in *italics* refer to illustrations.

A

acorns 30, *31*
advertisements 21, 191
aids *18*, 117, *117*, 119
    use of 119–122
all-purpose rug 106, *108*
amounts to feed 87, 164, 165
anti-cast roller 106, *106*
anti-sweat rug 103, *105*
apples 89
approach to jump 122
approaching a pony 11
artificial aids 117, 118, *118*
auction 21
automatic drinking bowl 153
automatic trough 29, *29*

B

back protector *137*, 142
bad habits 157, *162–3*
balance 115
ball and rope tether *155*
bandages 62, 110, *111*, 142–3
bandaging *61*
bang tail *130*, 131
barley 88
barley straw 85
barrel elimination 66
beans 88
bed, laying a 85, *85*
bedding 83, 85, *85*
belly clip 135, *135*
British Horse Society Assistant
    Instructor (BHSAI) 10, 170
bit, action of 36, 99
bit, position of 35, *96*
bits 95, 97–9 *98*, *99*
blanket 107, *107*
blanket clip *134*, 135
body as aid 117
body brush 46, 55, 66, 158
bogey time 142
bolts 83
boots, riding 60
bot-flies 71
bracken 30, *31*
bran 89, *165–6*
bran-mash 89
breast-girth 102, *102*
breastplate 102, *102*, 104
bridle *34*, 35, *35*, *37*, 94
bridle decoration 99
bridle hook 43, 46, *47*
bridling *48–9*

bridoon 98
browband 35, *35*, 99
brushing *111*
brushing boots *111*, 114, 142
buckets 47
bucket holder 83, 154, *154*
buckle guards 40

C

canter 15, *18*, 19, 119, *120*
cast 107, *155*
cavesson *35*, 36, *37*
chaff 89, 164
Chase-me-Charlie 63
cheekpiece 35, *35*
chinstrap *137*
clenches 58
clipping 131
clippings, grass and hedge 33
clothes, riding 59–60
clothing in competitions *136–7*, 142–3
clover hay 51
cold-shoeing 55
cold weather 54
combination jumps 129
combined training 143
companionship 30
competition, age limits 78
competition, types of 139
concentrates 88, *166*
conditioning 168
conformation 22, *22–5*, 25
coronet boots *112*, 114
coughing 74
cracked heels 54
crash-cap *137*, 142
crib-biting 157, 163, *163*
cross-country 139, *140–1*, 142
crupper 41, 102, *102*
cubes 88, 164
curb bit 98, *99*
curb chain 99
curry-comb 46, 54

D

dandy-brush 47, 54
day rug 103, *108*, *110*, 159
deadly nightshade 30, *31*
dealers 21, 175
decrease in pace 121
deep litter 85
diagonals *9*, 18
dismounting 13

double bridle 92, *95*, 142
Dr Bristol 98
dressage 142
dressage saddle 91, *92*
drop noseband 92, *93*, *95*, 142
droppings 85, 157

E

eggbutt snaffle 98
equine influenza 70
exercise for stabled horse 162
exercise rug 106
exercise (support) bandage 111, *111*, *113*

F

farrier 55, 174
feed, measuring 87
feed store 154
feeding programme 50, 51, 52, 54, 87–90, 164–6
feeding times 5, 90, 157
feet, care of 55
feet, picking up *55*
fetlock boot *112*
field 27
field shelter 29, *30*
finicky feeders 166
first pony, buying 20
    choosing 20–26
flash noseband 95, *96*
flat racing 171
flatwork 118
flies, protection from 54
French snaffle 98
front-unload trailer 183
food containers 156
forging *24*
full clip 131
Fulmer snaffle 98

G

gallop 15, 19, *19*, 121
galls 74
gamgee 111, *113*
gate 29, *29*
general-purpose saddle 36, *38*, 91, *91*
girths 39, 41, *41*
girth straps 39, 92, 103
gloves 60
goose-rump *23*
grakle 95, *96*
grazing 25
green food 164

grooming *53*, 54
grooming kit 46, *56–7*
ground line 127, *127*
gymkhana games 63, *64–5*, 66
gymkhanas 13, 63, 87

H

hair net 60
halt 121, *121*
hands as aid 117
handy pony 66
hat 59
hay 51, 87
    buying 52, 54
    storing 51
haynet 52
hay-rack 83
head carriage 22
headcollar 42, *42*
headpiece 35, *35*
head-shy 25
hock boots 110, *112*
hollow-back *24*
hoof *58*
hoof oil 47, *57*
hoof-pick 46, 54, 66, *57*
horse box 183
horse breeds 147
horse, choosing a 146–7
horse, costs of 146
horsehage 51
hot shoeing 55
hunt service 174
hunter clip *131*, 135
hunter conformation 147
hunter trials 139, 142
hunting 87

I

impulsion 116
increase in pace 121
injections 70
inoculation 70
insurance 182
Irish martingale 100, *100*
irons 41, *41*

J

jacket 60, *136–7*, 142
jewelry 60
jockey skull-cap 59, *137*

jockey strap 186
jockey training 171
jodhpurs 60
jump-off 67
jump, phases of 122, *122*
jump, types of 124, *125*
jumping 115
jumping classes 67
jumping course, building 127, *129*
jumping saddle 92, *93*
jumps, building 124, *123–7*
jute rug 103

K

kick bolt 83
kicking 163
knee caps 110, *112*
knee rolls *38*, 39, 92

L

lameness 74
laminitis 71, 72
landing after jump, 122, *122*, 123
laurel 30, *31*
laying a bed 85, *85*
lead-rope 42–3
legs as aid 117
lending a pony 81, 187
lice 71
linseed 89
linseed jelly 164
livery stables 167
loading 186
loose box 82, 151
loose-ring snaffle 98
lung worms 74
lunging *169*

M

maize, flaked 88
mane comb 47
mane plaiting *132*, 138
mane pulling 130
manger 154
martingale 100, *100*, 142
meadow hay 51
moment of suspension 122, *122*, 123

moulting 55
mounting 11, 13, *13*
muck heap 85
mucking out 85, 157
mud fever 54

N

narrow chest *23*
National Hunt racing 171
native ponies 22
natural aids 117
near side 11
New Zealand rug 62, 86, 106, *106*, *109*, 167
night rug 103, 159
noseband 36, *37*, 92, *96*
numnah 103, *103*

O

oatmeal gruel 89
oats 88, 164
oat straw 85
off side 11
oil drums as jumps 125, *125*, *126*
one-day events 142
overreach boots 111, *112*, *113*, 142

P

pad saddle 42
paces 15–19, *16*
pallets as jumps 126, *126*
panel 39
parasites 71
peat moss 85
Pelham bit 98, *99*
plaiting *132–3*, 138
plastic containers as jumps 126, *126*
points of horse *23*
poisonous plants 30, *31*
pole-cups 126, *127*
poll pad 110
Pony Club 59, 60, 78, 81, 87, 92, 142, 147,
   182, 187, 190
poor doers 167
position of rider 14, *14–5*, *17*, *115–6*,
   119, 122, *124*
privet 30, *31*
protective boots 111, *112*, *113*, 114
protective clothing for pony and rider 107, *109*, *110*,
   111, *137*, 142
putting on a rug 107, *107*

Q

quartering 157
quick-release knot 52, *52*
quidding 167
quilted rug *108*

R

racing 171
ragwort 30, *31*
rear-unload trailer 183
recovery after jump 122, *122*
red worms 71
rein back *121*, 122
reins 35, 99
reins, holding 14, *15*, *95*
removing a rug 107
resting horses 167
riding instructor 10, 170
riding schools 10, *12*, 19
roach back *24*
roller 106
roller pad 106
roots 89, 164
roughing off 167
round worms 71
roundings *97*, 99
rubber stops 100
rugs 103
    measuring for 103
running martingale 100, *100*, *101*

S

saddle, fitting of 40, *40*
    parts of 38, *39*
saddle flap 39
saddle horse *46*
saddle rack 43, *43*, *46*
saddle stuffing 38
saddler 175
saddling up *44–5*
safety stirrups *41*, 42
salt 89
sawdust 83
schooling 118, *123*
seat 14, *14*, 15, *15*, *115*, 116, *118*, 122
second pony, choosing a 78–9
seed hay 51
selling a pony 79, 81, 187
shallow chest *23*
shampoo 47
shelter 29
shirt 60
shoes 55, 72 *114*

short rack 158
show, how to enter 63
show-jumping 139, 142
show preparation 130
show, the day after 67
showing saddle 91, *91*
skull-cap 59, *137*
snaffle bit 35, 98, *98*
snaffle bridle 35, 92, 142
snow in hooves 54
speedicut boots *112*, 114
sponges 47, 55, 159
spring tree 38, *38*
spurs 118, 142
stable 82, *85*, 151, *160–61*
    doors 83, *83*, 151, *151*
    fittings 83, 153
    floor 152
    lighting 83, 153, *154*, *155*
    roof 152
    size 151
    ventilation 152, 153
    windows 152, *153*
stable, planning permission 82
stable routine 157
stable rubber 47, 159
stable vices 162 3
stable yard 153, *160–61*
stabling a pony 85
standing martingale 100, *100*
stirrup-bars 40, 91, 92
stirrup-irons 41, *41*
stirrup-leathers 41
    correct length of 11, *11*, 14, *14*, *123*
strapping 158
straw 85
strongyles 71
stud work 171
sugar beet 88, 168
summer sheet 103, *105*
surcingle 106, *137*, 142
sweat flap 39
sweat scraper 47
sweating 74
sweet itch 72
switch tail *130*, 131

T

tack, buying 42
    cleaning 43
tail bandage 62
    guard 110, *110*
    plaiting *133*, 138
    pulling 130
    trimming 130, 131
take-off at a jump 122, *122*, 123
tapeworms 71
teething 75
temperament 21

tendon boots *112*, 114
tetanus 70
tethering rings 154
throat lash 35, *35*
tie 60, 142
titbits *16*, 90
trace-high clip *134*, 135
trailers 183
    loading*184–5*, 186
    towing 183
    unloading *188–9*
travelling clothing 107, *107–8*
tree, saddle 38, *38*
trot 15–16, 119
trotting poles 123, *124*
trough 29, *29*
turn-out 135
turning out *12*, 33
twisted snaffle 98
tyres as jumps 127, *127*

V

vaccination certificate 70
vaulting *68–9*
veterinary nurse 175

veterinary surgeon *173*, 175
voice as aid 117

W

walk 13, 119
water 29
water brush 47, 55
weaving *162*, 163
Weymouth bit 98
wheat straw 85
whip 13, 118, *118*, 142
wind-sucking 163
wisp 158, *158*
wood-shavings 83
working hunter pony 139
working with horses 169
worming 71, 168

Y

yew 29, 30, *31*